TITUS LEE

CONNECTING
WITH DISCONNECTED
YOUTH

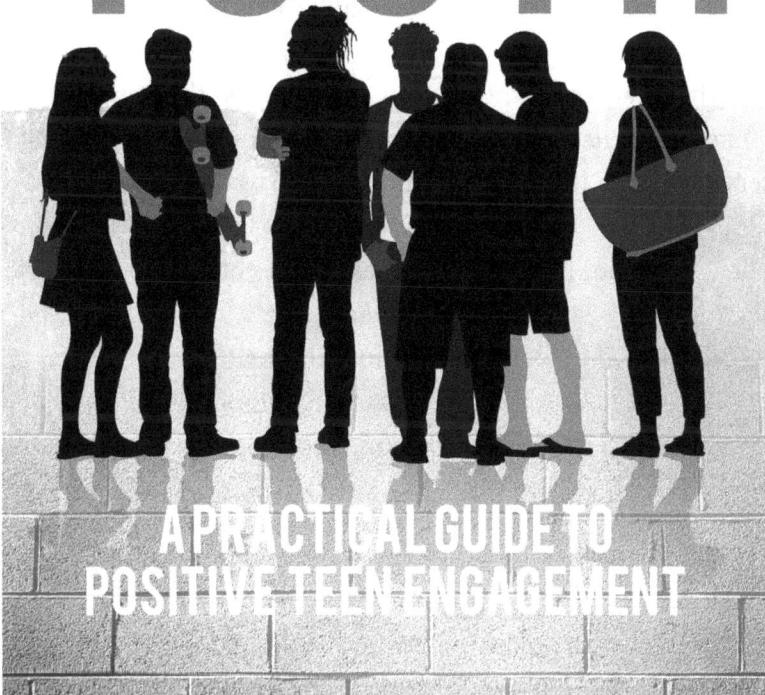

A PRACTICAL GUIDE TO
POSITIVE TEEN ENGAGEMENT

Connecting with
Disconnected Youth

© 2021 by Titus Lee

ISBN: 978-1-7361931-6-7

This is a work of nonfiction. To maintain their anonymity, some names have been changed in some instances, no characters have been invented, and no events have been fabricated.

For inquiries or to purchase copies of this book,
please contact us at:
Operation Link-Up Inc.
P. O. Box 437740 • Chicago, Illinois 60643
www.connection1000.com

DEDICATION

To the caring and courageous adults who have sacrificed countless hours to make a difference in the lives of youth in their communities.

Acknowledgments

I AM FOREVER INDEBTED to the people who have helped to shape my perspective and ignite my passion to reach teenagers. *Thanks, Dad and Mom, for prioritizing the importance of reaching youth in our home and ministry for as far back as I can remember. Mom, the Bible Club in our home made a huge difference in our neighborhood. Dad, the Boys Club at the church really mattered.*

Thanks to the late Dr. Marie Moody-James for seeing potential and possibilities in me and pushing me to reach teens when I was so young and barely starting on the journey in youth work.

I appreciate the awesome individuals who believed in my vision for Operation Link-Up many years ago when the organization began. Your support and service in the early years helped O.L.U. become what it is today. Many thanks to the late Marvin Ransom and the late Linda Williams. *Thanks, Lisa Bailey-Monegain and Kristina Young.*

Most of all, I am forever grateful to my beautiful wife, Nedra, with whom I shared my vision about reaching youth a few months after we began dating. *Through the years, you have been my glue, my confidante and my sounding board as I have evolved in this calling. Your dedicated service to Operation Link-Up has helped shape its mission for over twenty-five years. Words will never be able to adequately express my gratitude to you. I love you.*

Thanks to my three children, who have helped me practice what I preach as I've parented them through their teen years. *You are the apple of my eye, and I love you. Dranea, Faith and Titus, II, you are the best.*

CONTENTS

CHAPTER ONE

THE REALITY OF DISCONNECTION

IN A WORLD with unlimited ways to connect through technology, the question could be asked, "How is it possible for a teen in today's society to be disconnected?" With the myriad of handheld digital devices and social media platforms available, connecting is so easy. Nevertheless, we are often reminded by teen suicide statistics and angry students who perpetuate school shootings that being disconnected is very possible even when surrounded by people on social media platforms or as part of a video game tribe. Some teens known as "the life of the party" are disconnected. Some popular high school athletes are also lonely and disconnected. Some teens who attend youth camps and religious retreats still feel disconnected from their peers.

Connection is a more internal and emotional relationship than external and physical. Some teens have learned how to go through the motions of activity without any emotion... because their feelings have "died" as the result of disconnection. Hiding behind the mask of "likes" and "follows" on social media, involvement at church, performance in the classroom, and participation on the athletic field can be so easy for them. None of these associations in and of themselves are wrong; they are all positive preoccupations. However, finding out that young people can participate in some or all of these venues and still live with profound feelings of disconnection can be profoundly shocking for adults.

Some disconnected teens are totally "off the grid" and "under the radar." In other words, the true status of their emotional state remains undetected by the adults in their world. In aviation when an aircraft is "under the radar," it can't be traced or tracked. Utility services meters enable the utility company to obtain the correct measure of gas or electric usage. If the meter doesn't work, measuring the amount of usage is impossible.

Unfortunately, too many of today's teens are around adults who cannot correctly read how they really feel. The teens' true feelings are sometimes suppressed because they do not feel emotionally safe to genuinely express how they feel. Others are so numbed by hurt and disappointment, they have lost their ability to feel anything anymore. Many adults desire to make quality connections with teens. Knowing the various types of disconnection among teens is important to connecting with them.

THEY ARE DISTANT

As the result of being neglected, many times teens have a distant stare in their eyes. Sometimes they are present in body, but their spirit is absent. In fact, their spirits are oftentimes so crushed, bruised and battered, they have learned to cope by remaining in what I call "emotional hibernation." As a result, they have gone to sleep emotionally, thinking what they feel doesn't even matter. Hugging them is like embracing a hollow shell; shaking their hand reveals no meaningful grip. In all actuality, they are not there...but they are there. They are in survival mode, having retreated into tough emotional shells. These teens are sometimes experiencing emotional abuse, sexual abuse and/ or exploitation, broken homes (divorce), broken promises, rejection issues, deep-seated grief (over personal losses), and so forth. They have grown distant emotionally to protect themselves from further pain. These young people walk physically among us but remain far away from us emotionally.

THEY ARE DETACHED

These teens live in the margins of their "worlds" and our society, feeling they don't fit in anywhere. When some of them have tried to assimilate into certain circles, they have been rejected and rebuffed. They aren't deemed high enough in the social pecking order to be accepted. As a result, they function socially as "loose associates," often walking alone, sitting alone, and posting on social media alone.

Detached teenagers are the loners who feel unfit for meaningful friendships and relationships. They oftentimes press on silently through the pain of being left out. They are heartbroken as they do life alone on a daily basis. A large cross section of teens feels this way—like misfits. Their confidence and self-esteem suffer from being socially relegated by their peers to the status of "different, dumb and goofy." Many teens with unique needs, such as physical and/or learning challenges, live in this reality every single day.

THEY ARE IN DETENTION

Some teens live with constant rebuke. Whether at home or at school, their behavior seemingly warrants reprimand and restriction. However, a closer look at some of these teens will reveal that they lacked attention from key people early in their lives. That lack of attention has led to their present state of detention. Teen deviance is frequently a perverted cry for attention—even "negative attention." Sadly, domestic trauma, negative neighborhood circumstances, along with generational crimes and incarceration patterns within families, are frequently the root causes of teen detention.

The game of hockey has a special booth called the penalty box, where a player who violates some rule during the match is required to sit for five to ten minutes. While in the penalty box, the player can still observe the hockey game; however, he cannot take part in any of the action and help his team. The penalty box is the ultimate sports reality of "missing out"—being able to watch everyone else play the game but being unable to participate.

Some teens have become used to living in a "penalty-box" reality. They have grown accustomed to being disconnected from the mainstream of functional living and have accepted the "penalty box" as their plight. Being grounded at home, being assigned to the in-school suspension classroom at school, or being placed in the juvenile detention residence center has become their norm. They have become so used to missing out, they no longer feel any disappointment when they are excluded from meaningful student and community events. Many of these teens have incorrectly defined themselves by their behaviors and see themselves as "bad" and "no good." They sink deeper and deeper into the negative margins of society at incredibly young ages.

DON'T LET THEM DRY UP AND HARDEN

Many teens feel disconnected on a variety of levels. Subsequently, they have become hardened emotionally and difficult to handle at home, at school, and within their neighborhoods. I liken these teens to a partially or fully severed fingertip. Following the accident, only within a short amount of time, is reattachment possible. If the fingertip is detached for an extended period of time without being protected with ice, the skin tissue will die, and the nerves will be irreparably damaged. Furthermore, the fingertip will dry out and harden. A physician must reattach the fingertip to the finger before the tissue is irreparably damaged.

The sad reality is that far too many teens have "dried up and hardened" because they were detached from their emotions and society for too long. To cope with their disconnection, they have learned to suppress their emotions in an effort to no longer "feel." In actuality, they still "feel," but they have mastered the art of self-protection by masking their pain with hard, toughened attitudes and personas. Because they act out of their pain, they are often angry and on edge.

These teens are often described by their peers as being "crazy and uncaring." In actuality, they aren't crazy, and they do care. They are simply "acting out" of the pain and disappointment of being disconnected. Buried beneath these hard and tough exteriors are raw and tender hearts of young people desiring to build meaningful connections with their parents, pastors, and teachers. It is imperative for compassionate adults to work at fostering genuine connections with them before it's too late—before they dry up and harden. Remember, many of the young adults who are hardened today were once teenagers who were detached for too long.

CONNECT AND THEN DIRECT

Most youth instinctively desire meaningful connections with the adults in their lives. Sometimes the adults are the ones who need to upgrade their approach and their methods of interaction with today's youth. Adults can easily adopt an authoritative approach and disposition in their interactions with teens. After all, as adults we've been there and done that. We're not rookies who are just getting started. We've navigated life and dealt with its ups and downs. We know what's up! I think you understand what I'm saying. However, building meaningful connections with teens is not just about how much we know, who we know, and what we've accomplished. The real question is, are we open and interested enough in teenagers to put in the necessary time and effort to build a dialogue and earn their trust? Earning their trust is the foundation of making the connection with them. I say it this way: if there is no trust, there will be no connection; if there is trust, there will be a connection.

Many years ago, when I first became a youth pastor on the south side of Chicago, I took over a youth group numbering over 100 teens. I thought I was ready for action, and my initial approach was all about authoritatively giving the teens directions. On my first Sunday in the youth church, I told them what we were going to do, how we were going to do it, and what they needed to do. I was a young leader full of my own ideas and ideals. I came in calling the shots without any connection or credibility.

Many of the youth in the ministry had already been deflated by disappointment, abandoned by loved ones, and "hardened by the hood" in which they lived. Subsequently, many of them had trust issues with authority figures, particularly male leadership. They weren't really open to my talking to them and giving orders. Needless to say, my approach didn't work.

After six months of being the authoritative youth pastor, I clearly needed to change my approach because I wasn't getting through to the youth. I realized that I needed to humble myself, forgo being a know-it-all leader, and reinvent myself as a relational one. I did not need long to radically change my approach. I knew that making connections with them would require a considerable amount of intentionality on my part. Therefore, I started going to the local school and tossing footballs with students, playing video games with them, hanging out with them at amusement game centers, attending their games, and taking small groups out for impromptu pizza outings.

The atmosphere began to change almost instantly. As their trust for me increased, our youth group grew to almost 160 teens in the following three months. To my amazement, some of the youth who were initially the most resistant toward me became my mentees and welcomed my direction. I believe this acceptance was solely the result of my putting in the work of changing my approach and winning their trust, which eventually earned me the right to be heard.

Maybe you are where I was way back then. Perhaps you're trying to make inroads into the lives of your teens. I encourage you to search for the avenues and access points to their hearts. In other words, study them and listen to their interactions with each other. Hear about what they like, where they want to go, and what they want to do. As you learn about their interests, passions, and desires, use them as connection points. If you share some of their same interests, those mutual interests can become a common ground of connection between you and them. This approach will enable you to effectively engage them and build meaningful relationships with them.

The following are 15 areas of interest where adults and teens can connect:

1. Technology and computer devices
2. Music
3. Fashion
4. Sports
5. Entertainment

6. Culinary/Cooking

7. Video games

8. Performing arts

9. Audio and visual production

10. Religion

11. Automobiles

12. Home decorating and design

13. Drawing and painting

14. Fitness training

15. Nature and hiking

Use these points of interest, or others like them, as your initial premise of connection. Discuss them together, experience them together if possible, and share information with them about what interests them. You will soon discover that connecting with teens around shared, common interests will cause those who were once detached and distant to become re-attached. Making the effort and taking the time to forge these connections with teens will eventually provide the opportunity for you to give them direction and instruction when they need it in the future.

The next chapter will contain strategies on how to practically connect with teens by creating a connection culture. Whether you are a concerned parent, a youth minister or advocate, an educator or a coach, the tips included in the next chapter will help you go to the next level in your efforts to win the hearts of your teens!

THINK IT THROUGH

1. Do you know any young people who seem emotionally detached? If so, what attitudes have you observed in them?

_____

_____

_____

_____

2. How have you tried to build connections with the youth in your home and community?

_____

_____

_____

_____

3. Do you have any interests that you think could serve as a bridge to help you build relationships with youth?

_____

_____

_____

_____

CHAPTER TWO

CREATE A CONNECTION CULTURE

ENGAGEMENT IS EVERYTHING

FINDING WAYS TO positively engage teens enables you to build even stronger connections with them. Having intentional engagements with teens should be the priority of any person who endeavors to build connections with them. The word *engagement* means "to participate, become involved in, or to take part in." Unfortunately, adults oftentimes have accidental engagements with teens. Their interactions are derived from a need to instruct them, discipline them, or correct them. These engagements are frequently intense and one-sided. The adult usually assumes an authoritative position and says what needs to be said to the youth. These engagements are increasingly difficult for teens if the adult has made little effort to interact with them.

These forced, strictly instructional and disciplinary engagements leave a sour taste in the mouth of a teen. What is said by adults in these encounters is usually correct and necessary; however, teens sometimes see the confrontation in a negative light because of little to no engagement outside of those corrective contexts.

For adults to intentionally initiate positive teen engagements is particularly important. One way to initiate a teen engagement is to "relate and celebrate" teenagers as often as possible. If you are a part of the Baby Boomers or Generation X, this notion can seem absurd. I happen to be a member of Generation X, and I well recall that we teens were only celebrated when it was warranted. For instance, the norm for everyone in athletic competitions was not to receive ribbons. Only the top three finishers usually received congratulatory ribbons.

When I was growing up, a teen had to actually earn his celebratory moments through achievement. Our new looks and new clothes weren't widely celebrated by people because social media didn't exist in those days. Celebrations weren't quite as widespread and not nearly as expensive as they are now (i.e., proms, birthday parties, etc.). Our birthday parties in the 1980s were nowhere near as extravagant as those of today. Proms were not the expensive productions that many of them have become today. These celebratory events were considered privileges rather than entitlements. However, celebrations then and now are two entirely different notions. For adults to understand the importance of celebrating today's teens is imperative—even when it seems unwarranted and undeserved.

Buying in to the approach of celebrating teens may be difficult for many adults to embrace, especially when it's unwarranted. However, this approach is one of the more relevant ways to positively engage them because celebrating is the reality of our present-day culture. Recognizing their growth, progress, successes, efforts, technology upgrades, new approaches (hair, makeup, attire, etc.) and even their opinions is necessary. After all, they celebrate these various areas with their peers on a daily basis. If you are able to join in on the celebration of what matters to them, you automatically become more relevant in their "world of daily experiences." Your capacity to relate to them in a celebratory context is an important key to enjoying positive engagements with them. I know this concept may seem corny, even trite, but it's absolutely necessary!

Generation Z, i.e., those born between 1995 and 2015, oftentimes equate their value to how they are celebrated. I am certainly not saying that this metric is accurate, but it is frequently their reality. In recent years, the social media platform Instagram has skyrocketed in use among teens. Instagram permits them to post images of themselves on their wildly popular media platform. Their images, garnering likes and good comments (a form of celebration) often emotionally boost the young people who posted them.

Tik Tok is another social media platform that has enjoyed a meteoric rise in popularity. Tik Tok is like a modern form of karaoke with carefully created fifteen-to-sixty-second video vignettes streamed to viewers. Through Tik Tok, millions of teens are able to share their creative genius and fun moments. The videos receive likes with a simple double tab from the viewers. To teens, social media engagements like these are as real as in-person engagements. Their posts, pictures, or videos can garner anywhere from a few dozen to millions of likes and views. Parents and leaders need to know that our teens don't simply visit this "virtual world" occasionally; most of them live as "native citizens" in this world every single day. The need for celebration and recognition, which drives the social media narrative, is significant to teens.

The emotional and social construct of Generation Z is different than previous generations. They not only like to be celebrated, but they need to be celebrated; they thrive on it because it's natural to them. Therefore, adults who will positively engage them must be willing to celebrate them for the seemingly little things that weren't celebrated when they were growing up. Celebrating them is a form of positive engagement.

I liken celebrating them to depositing funds into a bank account. A depositor makes as many deposits as possible into the account so that when a withdrawal from the account is made, the balance doesn't go into the negative. Teens often resent adults who say absolutely nothing to them—until it's time to correct or direct them. They feel that they aren't engaged until something wrong needs to be addressed. Subsequently, when adults correct them (make withdrawals), the teens shut down and are emotionally closed because enough positive deposits haven't already been made.

We have all seen times when a teen turns his body away from an adult in disrespect or answers questions with cynical responses. In these instances, everyone involved feels disrespected. The adults usually feel that their position of authority has not been honored. The teens feel that the adults never have anything good to say to them. These intense adult-teen engagements frequently transpire in schools, ministries, and neighborhoods.

A sure way to avoid these negative confrontations is to give teens as much positive attention as possible. Make plenty of positive deposits into your teens—students, youth group members, and even teens in your neighborhood. Compliment them, notice their efforts, say something about their "fits" (outfits), so that when correction is necessary, the interaction won't become a negative engagement because of all the positive deposits you have already made.

INTENTIONAL POSITIVE ENGAGEMENT

For many years I led the 8th District Clergy Committee for C.A.P.S. (Community Area Policing Strategy). The 8th Police District was the largest in Chicago, encompassing over 80,000 residents. At that time, Mayor Richard M. Daley's desire was for the police districts to find ways to positively engage the teens in the city of Chicago. This intervention was desperately needed because the teens' only engagement with police officers was frequently negative. At that time, I served under John Kupczyk, the 8th District Commander. He and I put together a two-fold strategy in an effort to positively engage teens within the police district.

First, we targeted "hot spots"—troubled blocks where excessively high incidences of violence, gang activity, and drug trafficking took place. We decided to go to those areas and engage the teens and their families on Fridays and Saturdays.

On those two days, there were usually more police calls resulting from criminal activities. We would host cookouts, play music to attract the teens, play catch, pick up litter, pass out treats to the younger children, and simply hang out together. The clergy and police officers would lead these events. These initiatives were a form of positive youth engagement that helped to create a dialogue between the police officers and teenagers.

Secondly, in an effort to curb juvenile delinquent behavior on Friday nights, we conducted "late night sweeps." The police officers would identify youth who were out past the city curfew hours or engaged in negative behavior and bring them in to the district police station community room. There, the clergy and police officers would talk with the youth, play board games with them, and feed them snacks. We also provided them with literature about good community programs they could join on future Fridays rather than hanging out in violation of curfew hours. We would also call their parents or guardians, immediately explaining what had happened, and the clergy would frequently drop them off at home. So instead of the youth being brought in, written up, and detained at the 8th District Police Station until their guardian came to pick them up, we turned it into a time of positive engagement with teens.

The sole purpose of these efforts was to build rapport between the youth and police officers by facilitating positive engagement opportunities. This endeavor only happened through the intentional effort from the Chicago Police Department and Clergy Team. The clergy and police officers went out of their way to open lines of communication with the teens in the neighborhood. Whenever intentional positive engagements were conducted in hot-spot areas, a notable decrease could be seen in the tension that had sometimes previously existed between the police, the youth, and their families. These intentional engagements helped build meaningful connections and dialogue between law enforcement officers and youth. In this case, all that was needed was a little extra effort to engage the youth, and the plan worked.

HONK, HELLO AND HIGH FIVE

Recognition really matters to teens. Recognizing someone validates their presence. It's like saying, "I see you, and you matter to me." In the midst of a communication avalanche of social media, texting, FaceTime, and instant messaging, many teens still feel overlooked and unnoticed. Some teens from large families feel overlooked because of the lack of attention. Some who do not think they are as smart as their peers feel overlooked because of their grades or how they learn. Some who don't believe they are as cute or handsome as other teens feel overlooked because of their appearance.

I believe many teens engage in negative and risky behaviors because they feel overlooked and unnoticed. That lack of attention, whether real or imagined, causes scores of them to end up in detention. They act out of their "attention deficit," which often gets them into trouble. Sad to say, some teens would rather receive negative attention than no attention at all. For this reason, adults should proactively try to give attention to teens because some of them are starving for a person's care and consideration.

When the Operation Link-Up Program first moved to the Marquette Park neighborhood on the southwest side of Chicago, I knew no one. I decided to employ a simple strategy I call the "honk, hello and high-five" strategy. I would greet every teen I saw with a "Hello!" I would give high-fives to the guys and girls when I walked past them on the streets. I would honk my horn and wave at teens whenever I drove past them. Employing this strategy was my way of trying to recognize and engage teens in this new area.

Needless to say, some of them totally ignored me, while others looked at me as if I were crazy. Some of them politely smiled at me, while others fully engaged me with a wave, a high-five or even conversation. I knew to experience success in that area would require intentional recognition and engagement with every single teen who crossed my path. My simple recognition strategy worked! In fact, through the conversation that followed the hello, honk or high five is how most of the youth in that area were initially invited to our program.

A young man called Mario was one of the young men in that area who responded to my aggressive engagement approach. He would hang out across the street from my youth center in front of a liquor store. When I arrived at the youth center every morning, he would usually be there. He was always well dressed, wearing a pair of super-nice gym shoes. My relationship with Mario began with a wave and a morning "Hello!" every time I saw him. After a few months of waving and greeting him, I started walking across the street to comment on and compliment his nice clothing and shoes. My interactions with him were not contrived or fake; they were genuine. I soon discovered we both liked sharp clothing, which was my initial access point of connection and dialogue with him. Eventually the hellos and high-fives became hugs between us.

What I didn't know about Mario was that he knew "everyone" in the neighborhood. One afternoon he stopped me as I was walking and introduced me to a large group of his young buddies. He said, "This is Rev. Lee, and he's cool; he's all good." Within one month of his making that statement, he and several of his family members, as well as all of his buddies, became a part of the Operation Link-Up mentoring program! One quality connection with one guy linked me to so many youth in that part of the community. In a matter of weeks, the program grew from a few kids to being packed out with youth all because of the connection that I had built with Mario. His becoming my advocate and program promoter in the neighborhood all started from a hello and a wave every morning when I saw him.

I learned the following lessons from my honk, hello and high-five engagement with Mario many years ago:

1. If you connect with the "right" one, you will win his or her "world."

2. If you lead a youth program, going after teens and not quotas is important. Being driven by numbers is the wrong motivation and can make your engagement

with teens seem disingenuous. Instead, make sincere, genuine connections, and those connections will lead to organic growth in your program.

3. Assignments are sometimes intentional, but growth and numbers are unintentional. For instance, you may pour a great deal into one youth, not knowing that through that successful connection and the word-of-mouth advertising of that youth and his "world," i.e., parents, educators, and so forth, many others may be drawn to your program.

MOST TEENS ARE A CONNECTION AWAY FROM CONQUEST

The goals and aspirations of most teens will only be reached with the assistance of an adult who can speak into their lives and offer them guidance. In many ways, their spiritual, academic, and social successes are predicated on the counsel and care they receive through their connections with the adults around them. These connections are especially important; in fact, they are more like partnerships between an adult and teens. An effective partnership occurs when two or more people work together toward a common goal. For most teens, right connections and partnerships are all that they need to reach their potential. Teens are at their best when they feel connected to caring adults.

Understanding that teens desire to be a part of "someone" more than they do "something" is so important! In other words, they long for organic relationships that evolve in a sincere manner. Something *organic* naturally grows on its own. Just as organic plants grow naturally, teens also desire connections with adults that grow naturally. If the connection seems insincere and disingenuous, they will quickly lose interest and fade away. For that reason, these connections must be built for the right reasons. Educators and youth workers who serve teens on a daily basis must grasp this reality and connect with the youth they serve with genuine care and compassion—not from a sense of duty.

Dear friend, your work should be more than "just a job" to you. Working with teens is something you should feel called to do. Genuine care, compassion, and concern should flow from a great sense of feeling called to do what you do among youth. If you see your job as something that you have to do rather than something that you get to do, you will more than likely come across to your youth as half-hearted and insincere. Working with teens has to be more than a job to you; it must be a calling that compels you to forge connections with youth. Sincerity from adults is the glue that binds adult-teen connections together.

Teens want to know that their connections with adults are genuine and can be counted on. Instead of trying to connect so you can build program numbers, increase test scores, meet funding quotas, or create good photo opportunities, try your best to create a culture of genuine and organic connections.

Unfortunately, I've seen the fallout from adults initiating youth programs with wrong intentions. They seek to gain only for themselves and their organizations; theirs is not an effort to genuinely connect with the youth of that area or school. These types of programs frequently happen in large urban areas like Chicago. The adults show up, set up their programs, take pictures for future promotions and funding opportunities, stay long enough to institute their program, and then leave. In some of these instances, the youth are basically a "means to end" because they are treated like commodities.

Connecting with youth should be more than what we can get out of it; the focus must be about what we can give to them. Every youth program session, phone call, e-mail, house visit, outing, and mentoring session should be infused with sincere compassion and concern for them. Always remember that teens long for relationship over rhetoric. They are not really concerned about your doing your job so you can be compensated or grow your organization. What they really want is to be assured that your connection with them is genuine, real, and can be trusted. Make sure your efforts come from a heart of sincerity. Remember this, what comes from the heart of a sincere adult can connect with the heart of the most difficult and hard-to-reach teen!

Mrs. Barb Lipnick, my Spanish teacher in high school, had an incredible way of connecting with students. Obviously, her job was to teach us the Spanish language. However, when I would go to her class for tutoring, it was an amazing learning experience. I still remember her because she asked me questions about my day, discussed current events with me, and even asked me for my opinion about pop culture. Then we would start Spanish lessons. Her approach was incredibly effective because she had mastered the art of connecting with her students.

Yes, Mrs. Lipnick was a highly effective teacher of the Spanish language, but she was much more than a teacher; she was an incredible connector! I knew that teaching was more than just a job to her. I knew her concern for me as a person was genuine and authentic. Her approach motivated me to work a little harder, study longer, and do my absolute best in her class. All of these years later, I still admire her awesome ability to connect with students. The care and concern of teachers like her motivate students to be their best.

I know that many other teachers are like Mrs. Lipnick was, and I salute every one of them. *Thanks for taking the time to forge genuine connections with your students! Those connections inspire youth to be their best in your class. As the saying goes, people don't care how much you know until they know how much you care.*

Always remember that partnerships between adults and teens grow from the soil of sincerity and care. As you work with teens, it's important for them to know that they really matter to you. Be sure to connect in every way possible—discuss sports, fashion, technology, entertainment, and whatever else you can with them. Compliment them whenever you can. These intentional actions will grant you access to their world and give you authentic influence with them. Such interactions will never be time wasted. I liken them to pouring water on young trees. The more water you pour, the more the root system will thrive, and the more the tree will grow. Your connection with teens may very well be the difference between their success or failure. As they pursue their dreams and goals, your partnership with them will make all the difference in the world. Be sure to see these partnerships with teens in this respect: when they win in life, everyone wins. You also win because of your investment of sincere concern and care.

THINK IT THROUGH

1. How do you usually celebrate accomplishments of youth in your home, community, etc.?

_____

_____

_____

_____ ✑

2. If you were placed in an area where you didn't know any youth or families but desired to start a youth program, how would you go about building new connections in that area?

_____

_____

_____

_____ ✑

3. How can adults who work professionally with youth avoid burnout and remain motivated to serve youth each day?

_____

_____

_____

_____ ✑

CHAPTER THREE

NEVER BECOME NUMB

SOME PEOPLE COPE with difficult issues by closing up—
the ultimate avoidance mechanism. Some people ig-
nore all forms of media news in an effort to avoid bad news
and negative headlines. The twenty-four-hour news cycles
introduce new stories around the clock. Furthermore, many
people are exhausted and heartbroken over the negative news
about today's youth. Subsequently, they do their best to ig-
nore the harsh realities of school shootings, youth vaping, an
epidemic level of drug use, youth gang activity, and even the
obnoxious young people who hang out in their local malls.
Truly, the negative news about youth can be terribly depress-
ing. However, avoiding these realities doesn't make things any
better; it only makes them worse.

Some adults find it easier to evade the youth issues of their
communities rather than to address them. In an effort not to be
swallowed by the avalanche of bad news about youth, they simply
mind their own business. They endeavor to stay out of the way
of the rowdy, ruthless and unruly kids in the neighborhood. The
truth of the matter is that everyone is directly or indirectly af-
fected by the youth of their communities. Steering clear of them

doesn't help anything; it only adds to the disconnect that often exists between elders and teens in certain areas and organizations. Sadly, some adults have literally shut down their emotions when it comes to youth. They feel that trying to engage them in a meaningful manner is hopeless. Some adults cope with the ills and issues of teens by avoiding them completely.

The result of bad news usually being the big news is that the deviant and delinquent actions of teens are seemingly highlighted more often than their positive feats and accomplishments. When watching primetime news, the photos of young African-American and other minority men are frequently flashed across the television screen in association with criminal activities. This barrage of negative images and stories about them can make avoiding them seem rational. Steering clear of them can seem justifiable and the right thing to do out of an abundance of caution.

Just think: if you have limited interaction with a people group about whom you consistently hear negative information, adopting a negative attitude toward them becomes relatively easy. Becoming implicitly biased and prejudiced toward them based on what you hear and see is even easier. Believe me, bias and prejudice issues are not only racial; they are often generational—from elders toward youth.

Chicago is home to thousands of teenagers who study hard in school, are involved in extra-curricular activities, do chores in their homes, serve in their neighborhoods, work part-time jobs, and attend worship services with their families. The positive attributes and stories of these incredible young people are too often overshadowed by the negative actions of their troubled peers.

When I travel outside of Chicago on speaking engagements, people often ask me why the teens of Chicago are so violent. When answering that question, I often explain that in any geographical setting, there are teens who do right and others who do wrong. I explain that urban teens shouldn't be viewed monolithically but rather individually. I often add that Chicago teens are no different from the teens in smaller cities and rural areas. "All teens, regardless of where they live, desire to be loved, accepted, and secure. What must be understood is that there are no *bad* teens. There are *hurting* teens, *neglected* teens, and *violated* teens who frequently act out of their pain."

For adults not to uphold or defend prejudiced opinions about teens is so particularly important to engaging with these teens. Prejudice in this context is making conclusions prior to one's own experience or engagement with them. When this type of prejudice sets in, the heart becomes callous and insensitive toward youth.

THE NUMBING EFFECTS OF PESSIMISM

Some people contend with the physical challenge of neuropathy on a daily basis. The disease of neuropathy greatly limits the nervous system, causing numbness in the extremities of the body, such as the feet and hands. As a result of this numbness, people cannot feel physical touch or vibrations. This condition can severely alter their lives and limit how they experience physical sensations. The disease can progress and become so bad that the person cannot feel his toes or fingertips.

I have known a few people who have suffered with this disease. They have shared about the discomfort that neuropathy brought to their life. I knew some people who could see me reach out to take their hand, but they couldn't feel my hand touching theirs. I have always felt much sympathy in my heart for those dealing with this disease.

Sad to say, some people have emotional neuropathy like those who suffer from physical neuropathy. Having lost their empathy or compassion for the teens, these people can no longer feel anything toward them. They are often emotionally detached from the teenagers around them. Their emotional nerve endings have died, which results in emotional numbness. To be perfectly clear, you can actually be around youth on a daily basis and still lose your feeling for them.

This numbness can frequently be identified in the tone and tenor of some adult conversations. Their negative talk tears down teens without any sensitivity whatsoever. Their conversations start with statements something like the following:

- "These kids today are ridiculous…"

- "These kids are terrible…"

- "These kids get on my nerves…"

To a certain degree, I understand their sentiments. Today's youth do things I didn't dare do in the 1980s when I was in my teen years (at least I would like to think that…ha ha)!

However, the *"these kids are doing this and that"* are *our* kids! They are being reared in our homes, schools, and communities. We must always remember that they merely reflect the environments and experiences in which we have reared them. Therefore, we shouldn't speak pessimistically about them nor emotionally abandon them simply because we don't understand them. Pessimism sees the worst in them, and trust me, I know that's easy to do. However, we can't become so numb that all we can see is what's not right! We must remember that inside every teenager is a beautiful treasure that can only be seen through the lens of optimism and definitely not through the lens of pessimism.

Teens can feel the negative attitudes and undertones that come from pessimistic adults. The negativity of pessimistic adults is detectable in the most basic of interactions. For instance, when a teen is holding a conversation with a pessimistic adult, that adult will often talk at them rather than talk *with* them. When talking to teens, some pessimistic adults will even insult them or make snide remarks to them.

Teens seemingly have a "negativity radar" in their spirit because they can sense this pessimism almost immediately. They will, in turn, make statements like:

"That person really doesn't like me."

"That person is mean to me."

"That person never has anything nice to say."

Teens generally have very keen emotional sensitivities and can easily discern the difference between optimistic attitudes or pessimistic attitudes.

I am aware that adults must instruct teens in a firm manner from time to time. However, if an emotional base of negativity already exists in the heart of that adult, the words often come out in a harsh, unloving manner. The teen is left more wounded than helped. I know that a fine line exists between correction and censure. Sometimes parenting, educating, and coaching require adults to raise their voices or give direct and forceful admonitions. However, when these interactions come from hearts that have been desensitized by pessimism, the teens can't feel the love—even when the admonition is really meant in love.

As you coach, educate and minister to youth, do what it takes to keep your emotional nerve endings alive. Do not become numb to the cry of the teen. No matter how negative the attitudes and behaviors of teens may be in your home, school, or ministry, try never to become negative toward them. Burnout is easy. What you see and experience as you try to serve them in these settings can overwhelm your spirit. The incidences, issues, and crises you must walk through with them can be exhausting and frankly disappointing. Avoiding becoming jaded when you've done your best and given your all with no positive response requires great inner strength. In this context, a teen's refusal to respond in a positive manner to your love and service can be so disheartening.

However, during these low moments, you must be extra-sensitive to what's going on internally with them. Try to remember that they are "miniature adults," working through a myriad of emotions, inward and outward changes, and challenges they don't quite understand themselves. Therefore, not losing your capacity to feel them is vitally important.

At one time the question "Can you feel me?" was a major part of any conversation I had with a teen. That question meant "Do you understand or relate to what I'm saying?" The answer to that question is exactly what our teens still want to know after they underperform, miss the mark, or fall shy of our expectations.

The question they are asking in their hearts is "Dad, Mom, Teacher, Pastor or Social Worker, can you *feel* me? Are you still open to me, or have you closed your heart to me because I made a mistake?"

The only way you will be able to answer, "Yes, I can feel you" is never to allow pessimism and disgust to deaden your emotional nerve endings, regardless of what happens. Remain sensitive to their feelings and needs and don't lose touch with them.

THE NUMBING EFFECTS OF "NEVER MIND"

I've frequently seen exuberant new youth workers tell teens about the wonderful program they intend to implement in the near future. It's the "We're-going-to-go-here-and-there," the "We're-going-to-do-this-and-that," and the "We'll-have-the-most-fun-ever" type of spiel.

Anyone who has ever worked with teens has made similar statements or heard them. Unfortunately, much to the dismay of the new, excited youth workers, the teens usually don't "buy into" the promises and the hype. They look and listen with skepticism as adults try to sell them on how wonderful their youth program will be. In fact, their faces and body language usually say "Never mind."

The phrase "Never mind," which is usually used in a dismissive manner, signifies a shifting of the focus to something else. As much as most youth would like to lock into the promises of adults, they are often inclined to utter "Never mind" in their hearts because of past disillusionment and disappointments.

Years ago when people bought used cars, they would say they were going to "kick the tires" of the automobile. The idiom simply meant they were going to thoroughly inspect the quality of the automobile before they would buy it. Well, teens also like to "kick the tires" on adults who make promises to them! Before they buy in to the optimism of new teachers, ministers and youth workers, they want to know the person behind the promises.

- *Are they for real?*
- *Will they keep their word?*
- *Can I really trust them?*
- *Will they even be here in a couple of months?*

In many ways, teens are exactly like adults. Similarly to the way adults scrutinize zealous salespeople who seemingly promise them the world about the product they're trying to sell, teens become skeptical of well-intentioned people who make big promises. Like adults, they feel that it's easier for them to say "Never mind" and keep their hearts closed to adults who make promises rather than open up to them and later be disappointed by their lack of follow-through.

Well-intentioned adults should realize that the negative responses of teens in these situations aren't personal; they are employed for emotional survival. So many teens have been let down by adults who broke their promises. Some adults didn't show up after promising that they would. Other adults disappeared into thin air...I call these *unexplained exits*. The heartbreaking realities of parents who are missing in action, youth ministers who suddenly leave after extremely short tenures, and mentors who fade after one or two get-togethers cause many teens to become wary and suspicious of adults who want to engage them. They erect high walls around their hearts in an effort to avoid more letdowns and disappointments.

You should not become hurt or offended by the dismissive attitudes teens may have toward you when you initially attempt to engage them. They may look at you funny. They may wave you off. They may show no gratitude for your sacrifices for them. They may rebel against all of your directives. They may even stand you up by not showing up. Don't let these actions get under your skin. Remember that they are doing what adults do when they "kick the tires." They are trying to figure out if your love is for real. They are trying to figure out if you will be there for the long haul. The key to winning them in these scenarios is to keep on loving them. Don't let your pride or ego get in the way of your loving them. Be like a persistent salesperson and don't let their objections stop you. Keep on showing them consistent love and care even when they are "tripping." Your diligence during these times speaks much louder than your words.

Working with youth is similar to sales in this respect: if you

CONNECTING WITH DISCONNECTED YOUTH

can overcome the objections, you can close the sale! I have seen too many adults wounded by teens because the adults didn't understand this point. I've seen some of them take teen objections personally, which resulted in their returning insults to the teens they were trying desperately to reach. I've seen well-intentioned adults speak bitterly to the very teens they were attempting to help because they had been hurt by the teens' responses. Some of them literally returned the very rejection they had experienced from the teens back toward them. These adults became numbed by the "never-mind" attitudes of the very teens they had set out to help. This hurt should never happen.

Never dismiss them because they reject your overtures and efforts to engage them. Your love has to be expansive enough to cover their faults. Remember this statement which also applies to teens: *hurt people hurt people.* Some teens have been so deeply wounded by previous disappointments that they will initially object to any adult who tries to show concern for them. Keep in mind that perhaps they have already had "bad sales experiences" with adults. If they look at you skeptically as you talk with them, don't let it bother you. Instead, be determined to win them over. Please don't bawl them out or block them out if you experience this type of resistance.

I encourage you to remain faithful in your efforts to build connections with them. They will eventually realize that your love is real! They may need a year to watch you in order to warm up to you and accept you as genuine. If so, that's okay! Don't lose your empathy and compassion for them during the process. Be like the salesperson who keeps calling after they have been hung up on and showing up after doors have been slammed in their face. Somehow, these salespeople muster the energy to call or knock one more time. Dear adult, you must be the same way. Don't let their "never minds" stop you or cause you to fade away from them. Some teens expect that to happen anyway. Keep showing up to their games, keep doing thoughtful things to encourage them, keep calling them once in a while, and eventually they will buy into you because you remained consistent in your efforts.

MAXIMIZE YOUR EMOTIONAL ASSETS

If you desire to connect with teens, maintaining your capacity to feel is important. Trust me, your capacity to feel really matters. I often say that if you can *feel* them, then you can keep it real with them. I don't wholeheartedly subscribe to what people call the "generation gap." In many ways, the concept is highly overrated, over-hyped and even mythical. Of course, differences exist between the generations. Styles change, interests change, and values even change generationally.

The basic needs of today's teens mirror those of today's adults. They want to feel loved, they want to experience security, and they want to be accepted—just like adults. Therefore, for adults to show empathy toward teens is the great equalizer in adult and teen relationships, helping to bridge generational divides. For this reason, it's imperative for adults who endeavor to engage teens to remember the challenges, troubles, and difficulties they experienced when they were teenagers. The ability to bridge that gap enables them to relate to teens more effectively regardless of the age differential. I call this ability "tapping into your emotional assets." An *asset* is "something that's valuable or useful." Your breadth of experience is your greatest asset when it comes to connecting with teens. Your experiences should give you a sense of empathy in your heart. If you can remember the stages of what you went through in wanting to be accepted, needing to belong, and desiring to feel loved, then you have what it takes to connect with today's teens. These memories alone, whether positive or negative, create parallels to help you relate to them.

Displaying empathy is crucial when you are trying to build connections with teens. Compassion and warmth transcend generational distinctions that would otherwise make it difficult for adults to relate to teens. Empathy enables you to understand them because you indirectly share in what they are presently experiencing and feeling. Always remember what it was like when you were "where" they currently "are." Your ability to connect to your past experiences enables you to reach them regardless of your age because your empathy for them easily erases the generation gap. I say it this way, you are old enough to direct them but young enough to connect with them (in spirit and attitude)! Your age doesn't disqualify you from reaching teens as much as losing your ability to *feel* them does. Therefore, whatever you do, don't let your emotional nerve endings die because your capacity to "feel them (their plight and pain)" means you will always be able to keep it real with them!

Think It Through

1. Why do you think some adults have negative attitudes toward youth?

_____

_____

_____

_____

2. Have you ever been on the receiving end of youth with whom you were trying to engage being dismissive of you because of their trust issues? If so, how did you try to win them over?

_____

_____

_____

_____

3. What helps you maintain empathy for the youth around you?

_____

_____

_____

_____

CHAPTER FOUR

FIVE WAYS TO WIN THEM

O PPORTUNITIES FOR US to win teens arise on a daily basis. When I use the term "win teens," I'm really referring to making significant enough inroads in their lives that you are able to influence their attitudes and actions. Another way of saying it would be to "win them over." Many of our teens have been lost to the deviance and delinquencies of the streets. Others have been lost to anti-authority attitudes; therefore, they rebel against all authority figures in their lives. Some have been lost to low self-worth.

A significant cross-section of teens has been lost to dangerous dependencies and addictions. For adults to build connections with teens in the home, the school, and the ministry has become increasingly difficult. Unfortunately, in some cases, the connection never existed. As a result, this gap will only be bridged when adults commit to forging meaningful connections with teens in their homes and communities. In this chapter, I will address five ways for adults to connect with teens, regardless of context. These strategic steps have been essential and extremely useful in my youth work through the years.

All five ways of building connections are important. However, utilizing these ideas may transpire differently from adult to adult. These five steps frequently take place in stages over a period of time. For instance, the "taking-an-interest" stage may be three or four months, or that many months may pass before you have a meaningful conversation with a teen. They must feel comfortable with you before they will share their feelings, cares, and concerns. Connection-building is different for everybody. Therefore, be sure to keep a pace that is best for you. Trying to rush from the "invest-in-them" stage to the "inspire-them" stage a few days after you make your initial connection with them is unnecessary and likely fruitless. When you are trying to win teens, it's important for you to pace and not race. As I said in the previous chapter, teens need long-term connections with adults for trust to really be established. Find the rhythm that works best for you and the teen or group of teens you are trying to reach and then walk out this five-step process over whatever period of time it requires.

The following are the five stages or ways for you to win teens in your home and community.

TAKE AN INTEREST IN THEM

Understanding that *interest* in teens precedes *instruction* to teens is vital. Sometimes adults easily assume an authoritative posture without any prior engagement. Adults sometimes take the "I-have-been-there-and-done-that" approach when trying to connect with teens; however, that disposition usually doesn't work. So many youth are dealing with trust issues; therefore, they often find it difficult to respond to being constantly told what to do by a well-intentioned adult who has shown little interest in connecting with them outside of the moments when they give them instructions.

Dear friend, instead of posturing yourself as the "know-it-all" adult who is supposedly there to "help them" by telling them what to do, try to flip the script. Why not clear some time from your schedule to spend some time learning about them? Be intentional about leaving your world and "going to their world." Schedule a Saturday away from what interests you, "go to their world," and do what interests them. Walk the mall with them, take them to their favorite eating spot, or catch a "can't-miss" new movie with them. Why not try this over the course of a few weeks? Make the time to show genuine interest in them. If you do so, it will be the beginning of winning them. Don't do it with an ulterior motive; rather, spend time with them because you genuinely want to establish or strengthen your connection with them. I call this process "seeds without strings," which means you show an interest in them regardless of whether or not they bring home A's or choose to join your after-school program or youth group.

Showing a genuine interest in them creates lines of communication and/or causes them to open up. Remember that many teens are attention-deprived; subsequently, they long for healthy engagement with parents, educators, and youth workers who make them the center of attention. They desire for adults to take a genuine interest in who they are and what they like—not just in what they do or fail to do. In fact, the way for to you be able to change or modify their behavior lies at times in your ability to learn about them as you take an interest in them. This step leads to the next step of investing in them.

INVEST IN THEM

Giving teens your ear is one of the most validating gifts you can offer a teenager. Whether they are in your home, neighborhood, school, or church, it's important that you listen to them. Many of them have feelings that often go unheard, and they feel ignored and unheard. The feeling of being unheard is often the root of their frustrations. We have too often seen the heartbreak that has been caused by teens who have felt ignored and unheard. Some of them have lashed out through school shootings, vandalism, public rants, and other disorderly behaviors.

Some teens who feel ignored engage in what I call the "notice-me" walk. The teens stroll slowly across an intersection or public walkway while the drivers in automobiles have to, in essence, *notice* them as they deliberately saunter in front of them. These behaviors are often the symptoms of teens who really need to be heard by adults. I believe that the risky, rude, and rowdy behavior of many teens is really their speaking in sociological sign language to the world. Much of this aggressive behavior equates to their pleading, "Hey, adults! Please *see* me. Please *notice* me. Please *listen* to me."

I often say that if you to listen to a teen for an hour, he or she will listen to you for the rest of their lives! I believe that and have seen the evidence of that truth among teens on the south side of Chicago for many years. You don't have to force conversations with them; simply give them permission to talk and let the narrative naturally evolve. You will soon realize that many of them are "bubbling brooks." Once they open up, they are like gushing streams of water, flowing from one topic to the next. The following suggestions are some practical tips that can help you to effectively listen to teens:

1. They will only share what's going on with them when they feel they can trust you.

2. Once they start talking, try to listen with minimal interruption.

3. Don't dominate the conversation.

4. Don't use what they say against them in any future interactions.

5. Try not to be judgmental toward them even when your opinions differ.

6. Watch their body language and listen to their tones and inflections in an effort to really try to understand the points they are trying to make.

7. Keep a straight face when listening because any negative facial expressions may cause them to shut down.

8. Be sure to hold what they say to you in confidence (as long as it is legally possible to do so).

The investment of listening to teens can pay the huge dividends in our homes, schools, and communities. When you listen to them, you can often hear the why behind what they do. You are able to hear their rationale and reasoning as they share their sentiments with you. In this context of listening, teens begin to trust adults. Most of them simply want to be heard by the adults around them; that's all. They know you will not agree with them on everything, but they do desire to be heard. A muzzled teen is usually an angry teen whose anger frequently comes out "sideways" through negative behavior at home and school. Therefore, teens must feel safe enough with the adults around them to let off the steam of what's really going on inside of them.

Listening—really hearing their teens—is one of the greatest investments that parents, educators and ministers can make. Listening to them gives you inroads so that you may positively influence them. Teens will be so open toward you after you have demonstrated openness toward them through simply listening to them. In a nutshell, if you listen to them, they will listen to you, which will enable you to talk them down, talk them through and talk them out of difficult and/or destructive scenarios. You will also be able to talk them into good choices and positive opportunities. Be sure to make the investment of listening to the teens around you; simply using your ears really works.

INVITE THEM

Teens often grapple with the following question: *where do I fit in?* Some of them have been excluded from the social circles of their peers. Others are distant from their families. Therefore, finding a place to fit in is of paramount importance to them. They desire to be included. Therefore, you must understand the power of an invitation. An invitation communicates so many messages, including:

"You matter to me!"

"I like being around you."

"You are accepted."

When you ask a teen to go somewhere or to do something with you, it is a big deal. Ultimately, you are saying, "You are welcome in my space. Regardless of your flaws and shortcomings, you are welcome!" Welcoming teens has a profound effect on them. To them, feeling welcomed equates to being accepted.

I have already alluded to the fact that teen rejection issues are rampant. Many of them have experienced the pain of being rejected by their parents. This rejection is a reality among many teenage boys who do not have regular, healthy interactions with their fathers. In fact, some of them have never had an adult male authority figure in their home. This sad reality has caused many of them to be open to any invitation from older males—even negative influences. Subsequently, these young men tend to relish the feeling of being noticed and invited into the "worlds" of older men. If the intent of the older men is negative, their invitations can have devastating effects on young men.

If fathers have been consistently absent, youth will gravitate to "father figures" who, at times, have nothing positive to offer these young men. Of course, this isn't true in all cases. I have witnessed attention-starved young men hide firearms, hold drugs, skip school, or join gangs at the invitations of men on the streets. I have seen these invitations lead these attention-seeking young men into school truancy, drug trafficking, and gang affiliation. The reality is, some youths would rather accept an invitation into a world of lawlessness and crime that they know is wrong than not to feel welcomed anywhere. Since all invitations are not good or wise to accept, how much more important it is for caring adults to make time to invite teens into positive environments and activities that will empower them.

May I encourage you to invite teens into your world? After you establish rapport with them by showing an interest in them and making the investment of listening, extending an invitation to them to join your world should be easy. Follow the important safeguards of parent/guardian notification and permission. Try to have another adult with you or invite two or more teens to avoid one-on-one situations. Invite them to join your family for dinner. Invite them to a neighborhood festival or gathering. Invite them to a worship service with you. Invitations like these can foster a sense of belonging in those who struggle with loneliness and detachment issues. These invitations will say more than you can say with a thousand words. These invitations will convey this message without your having to say it: "Your presence matters to me, and it's cool being around you."

Years ago I was introduced to a young man named Damon who was eleven years old. Although he was too young to be in our mentoring program, I immediately invited him to join. He initially connected with Operation Link-Up by attending summer day camp. The following school year, he became a part of our after-school programs. After a few months, I noticed that Damon would show up whenever he saw the lights on in the youth center. It did not seem to matter to him if the teen programs were in session or not; he would just show up. Sometimes I would be the only person there, and he would ask to come in for a few minutes and sit silently. He would usually ask me for a few pieces of paper to draw on, and then he would leave. This sequence would happen week after week.

As time passed, he became a fixture in our after-school program. Since he always wanted to hang close to me, I invited him to come to church with my family and me. He would always say "Yes" and come. Whenever I invited him to McDonald's to eat chicken sandwiches and burgers with a small group of boys, he would always come. I soon realized that wherever I was, Damon was...whether or not he was invited!

When Damon decided to open up and tell me about the rejection he had experienced all the way back to the time of his birth, his actions began to make sense to me. His father never accepted him as his child, and his mother struggled with addictions. He was sent to Chicago to be reared by his grandmother. A few times Damon would open up and talk to me about the deep disappointment he felt at never being around his father and mother. Sometimes tears would fill his eyes, and anguish would be written on his face as he described how badly the rejection made him feel. Several times he had high hopes of going to California to see his mother, only to have the plans cancelled at the last minute.

As I heard more and more of his story, I realized why Operation Link-Up was so important to him. Here was a place where he had never experienced rejection; his presence was always accepted, celebrated, and welcomed. He always had an open invitation to come to the youth center programs or just drop in. He was welcome at any time! As I reflect back on those years, I realize that Damon never once turned down an invitation to join me. One of my last invitations to him during his teen years was to go to a clothing store to pick out an outfit for senior prom. We had an incredible time matching up the suit, shirt and tie!

Who knows how many young men and women just like Damon would be thrilled to receive an invitation from an adult they respect? Why not take the time to invite them into your world? Be that positive influence on a fatherless boy or motherless girl who longs for acceptance. Your invitation to join your family for a meal, to take in a movie, or to play ball could have an indescribable impact on them! Your invitation will say more than you could ever say with your mouth. Your overture will communicate this fact: "I accept you, and you are welcome here." Look for the loners and try to invite them into your world. They are always grateful whenever a concerned, trusted adult says, "Come on, and go with me." Your invitation will open the door for you to become an inspiration to them.

The following are some tips on inviting teens into your world:

1. Try to avoid one-on-one situations as much as possible (unless they are family).

2. Don't pressure them to talk or to engage with other people they may not know when they join you. Some teens will just soak it all in, needing to be comfortable in that setting before opening up.

3. Always be accountable to their parent/guardian.

4. Only invite them into settings with family themes.

5. Help them feel at ease when they join you in settings that are new to them.

Inspire Them

One of the best gifts you can give to teens is an experience that help them to discover their passions. Of course, this requires the exploration of various environments. Exposing teens to environments that excite them and ignite them is so important. These types of experiences motivate them to strive to reach higher levels of achievement and excellence. If they never have had an "igniting experience," it's highly probable that they will underperform in many areas because of the lack of motivation. A youth's becoming passionate about the right things can be the difference between his success and failure. Try to take the teens in your life on journeys of discovery. Try to stretch their minds beyond their familiar world. Introduce them to new environments and experiences that pique their interests and cause them to ask questions.

The flames of many teens are flickering as the result of the lack of exposure. Some of them have become entrapped by the limitations of what is familiar to them. For example, many teens in urban areas rarely venture beyond a four- or five-mile radius of their homes. The same is true of some teens in rural areas who rarely venture beyond their remote settings. Both of these scenarios can be debilitating to their passions because they only see the world through the narrow lens of familiarity. The lack of exposure causes many teens to fear anything different from what they have previously experienced. Students are often unmotivated in school because they feel trapped in systems and cycles of failure. Subsequently, they fail to dream and strive for greater because they haven't been exposed to greater possibilities.

I have no qualms with teens desiring to excel athletically or entering the world of entertainment. However, sometimes one of these two areas is the only option they feel they can achieve. You ask some of them what they plan on doing as an adult, and they will say, "I want to be a professional basketball or football player or a rapper/producer." On the surface, these goals might sound good, but beneath these statements lie deep psychological conditioning that causes them to feel that they can only excel on the court, in the field, or behind the microphone. Sadly, too many teens feel this way. I am not against these professions because many athletes and entertainers have a positive impact on communities. However, too many teens feel they can achieve only in these areas. Therefore, exposing them to other possibilities is so important.

Exposing teens to new realities will help them to learn about what's really deep down inside of them. Therefore, be intentional as you introduce them to new places, new faces, and new opportunities. Ideally, exposing them in person is best, but if that's not possible, show them through movies, videos, websites, and books. Pay close attention to the questions they ask as a result of being familiarized with new areas. Take note of what they desire to experience again or the places they don't want to leave because of their enjoyment. These places and experiences may be potential points of passion for them. Try to figure out what environments ignite their flames of passion and try to continually expose them to those places.

Years ago I would take several teens from Operation Link-Up to an assisted-living facility to serve the elderly residents on Saturday mornings. The majority of the group who would go to serve were young men between the ages of twelve and fifteen years old. They would play board games with the folks, help them clean their rooms, and push some of them down the hallways in their wheelchairs. My hope was for these service trips to ignite a passion in the hearts of my youth to honor their elders by serving them.

Those service trips did, in fact, ignite the passion of one of our young men named DaShon. I was very pleasantly surprised to learn that he took the initiative to return to that facility by himself to serve the elderly outside of our bi-weekly Saturday morning visits. He would go there to assist the activities director every week. He did it so passionately that he was eventually hired as a teen to work at that facility. You see, DaShon already had the gift to help people in him. However, the exposure to that environment took his passion to serve people to a higher level! He is a great example of the impact an inspired teenager can make in a community!

The following are a few ways you can inspire teens:

1. Take them to the library for study time with the promise of their favorite meal afterward.

2. Take them to a college, semi-pro, or professional game to expose them to the hard work of next-level athletes.

3. Even if they are impoverished, take the teens to serve elderly, disabled, and impoverished people to learn the importance of selfless service.

4. Take them on a higher education trip to a college campus.

5. Take them on a day trip to a leading business corporation in your city or region.

6. Take them to the best restaurant possible to expose them to culinary excellence and next-level etiquette.

7. Take them to a religious teen worship service or retreat to expose them to next-level faith.

8. Take them to local museums and art galleries in your area.

9. Take them to creative arts workshops to help inspire their writing and lyrical skills.

———

10. Take them to a local radio or television station to see great audio and visual production.

You can expose teens to many other places in an effort to inspire them. Begin brainstorming about new ways to help the teens around you to discover their passions.

INSTRUCT THEM

Teens really desire to receive advice from the adults in their lives. They respond most favorably to adults they feel genuinely care for them. Therefore, by showing an interest in them, you actually build a platform from which you can instruct them, which is why I previously stated that interest precedes instruction. Teens readily hear adults who they feel have earned a right to be heard. Sometimes earning a right to be heard is simply listening to them in order to understand them. When that happens, they see you as credible and trustworthy because you care. Try to consistently hear them out as often as possible so they will open their ears to hear what you have to say.

There are multiple ways to positively instruct teens without badgering them and preaching at them. They respond best when directives are given to them in a way that's easy for them to understand. You may need to answer their questions about your directives. For adults from my generation (Generation X), we were instructed quite differently as teens years ago. We were told what to do, and we were expected to do it without any backtalk or questions asked. During those times, most adults didn't feel inclined to make sure we understood what we were told to do, whether it was at home, school, church or any other place. You were simply expected to do what you were told to do; that was the end of it. Our feelings didn't factor in to how they instructed us.

As a result of this style of communication, many Generation X and older Millennials have given our teens the green light to ask questions and express themselves about practically everything—including instructions and directives. Our youth have been reared in environments of open dialogue and the expression of their unfiltered feelings, primarily on social media as well as other forums. They expect to be heard as well as to be able to question what they don't agree with or understand. They are indeed the "conversation generation." Therefore, the "just-shut-up-and-do-it" authoritarian approach to communication from previous generations isn't always the best approach, nor is it relevant these days. For adults to build relationships with teens so they can leverage their established connection when they need to give them directions is far better. When this is the case, adults can more easily give directions without having to make demands because of the established connection. The key to getting teens to do what you want and/or need them to do is keeping a constant dialogue with them so when instructions are given, they are more responsive.

The purpose of instructing teens should be constructive—not destructive. When issues arise, you really need to correct, remember to focus on the issue that needs correction, and never make it a personal attack. Always remember that the objective of instruction is to build them and never to break them.

Therefore, instructions should always be given to teens in love and compassion. Their intelligence and potential should never be diminished and insulted in the process. As you critique, correct, and challenge the teens in your life, do so with sensitivity, strength, and sincerity. You will succeed every time!

You can instruct the teens around you using the following three methods:

1) Critique Them.

Speak to them about what interests them, such as performances, social media posts, or hobbies. Talk with sensitivity and tell them how you think that they can improve or do better.

2) Correct Them.

Confront them about their actions or lack of thereof in areas of importance such as academics. Sometimes their efforts are far below their potential, and your words can spur them to excel in the areas where they have previously underachieved.

3) Challenge Them.

Identify something you are confident that a teen can achieve with extraordinary and diligent effort, and then challenge him or her to go for it. It may be spiritual, academic, social, athletic, etc. I believe challenging them is a great way to motivate them to be their best.

THINK IT THROUGH

1. How have you previously engaged youth? Have you "gone to their world" or invited them into "your world"? What did you learn through these engagements ?

_____

_____

_____

_____&

2. What are some methods you can use to inspire your youth in the future?

_____

_____

_____

_____&

3. Can you think of a teenager who would welcome your critique, correction, or challenge? What has brought your relationship to the point of their being open to your advice and input?

_____

_____

_____

_____&

CHAPTER FIVE

THE POWER
OF YOUR PLATFORM

PAIN IS PART OF YOUR PLATFORM

DON'T UNDERESTIMATE THE value of your past experiences. Accept and own them because they are valuable. In fact, the adults who sometimes are able to engage youth most effectively are the ones who would have seemed the least likely to be able to do so during earlier stages of their lives. More often than not, these effective adults don't stand on platforms of fame, fortune, and celebrity. Many times they stand on their own platform of what they have survived. Some of them struggled with their own rejection issues, eating disorders, disabilities, emotional abuse, sexual abuse, feelings of abandonment, low self-esteem, suicide attempts, academic failures, criminal backgrounds, poverty, drug dependency, or sexual promiscuity. Right now they look nothing like what they have been through because they have learned how to walk victoriously in areas where they once suffered defeat.

If you have survived any of these issues I mentioned in the previous paragraph, you are blessed! The fact that you survived those ordeals shows that you have been preserved for a greater purpose. Sadly, some people become so entangled in issues like these that they are never able to progress beyond those painful experiences. For you to know that your future will be awesome is of utmost importance. I am certain that what you survived will enable you to greatly impact the next generation. If you have been wondering why you had to endure so many hardships in your younger years, please know that you were being prepared for right now. Those experiences, however painful they may have been, have literally created a platform for you to love, comfort, and encourage today's teens.

Don't pity yourself because of your past pain; rather, process it correctly. Understand that the pain has literally set the stage for you to help teens who surround you on a daily basis. What you endured during the earlier seasons of your life increased your capacity to connect with teens who are struggling with those same or similar issues now. Suffering is significant because it increases your ability to identify with hurting youth.

Boldly stand on the platform of your past pain and peril by not dismissing or downplaying what you went through because those experiences have helped to fashion you into the person you are today. Try to free yourself from asking why certain things had to happen to you; rather, see those experiences as the building blocks of your platform so they make more sense to you. As you accept and resolve your own painful experiences, you will be able to effectively engage youth who are going through those same experiences now. However, if you haven't reconciled your own painful matters in your mind, the present issues of some teens could end up triggering your own unresolved issues and cause you to regress backward into your own unresolved matters.

I've seen youth workers who were still in pain regarding their own issues become emotionally overwhelmed by teens who were experiencing similar ordeals. I know of some adults who quit doing youth work because of these types of scenarios. They were not yet healed enough to help teens. Their souls were so wounded that they really couldn't be of benefit to the youth they truly desired to help.

If you have had a painful past, you must acknowledge the pain, accept it, and seek out ways to pass on to the next generation the wisdom you acquired from these ordeals. One of the hardest but most liberating truths to accept is that there was purpose in your past pain. Understanding that truth can help bring healing and closure to the deepest wounds of your soul.

Accept your past as preparation for your present platform. Whether you are a teacher, a pastor, a social worker, or a coach, remember that every predicament of your past had a purpose. If necessary, talk through the hurts with a trusted person, pray about the issues surrounding your hurt, and even seek counseling. Taking these steps can help you bring closure to the open and unresolved issues of your heart. When your heart is healed, you will be able to more effectively pour out compassion and comfort to the hurting youth in your home, neighborhood, and school. Seek out personal closure regarding your past pain because it makes all the difference in the world.

I'm reminded of the Bible story of Joseph, who was a dreamer. During the early years of his life, he was abused, abandoned, and sold into slavery by his brothers. He became the leading employee of his slave master, only to be falsely accused of attempted rape by his master's wife. This false accusation brought him an unwarranted prison sentence; thus, he spent many years in prison for a crime he did not commit.

While in prison, he used his God-given extraordinary gift to interpret the dreams of his fellow inmates. The word spread about his dream interpretation ability, which eventually opened the door for him to stand before the king of Egypt and successfully interpret the king's dream. Immediately thereafter, he was promoted into the second highest political position in Egypt. He was lavished with honor, riches, and the best of that kingdom. The promotion from prison to the palace seemingly happened overnight, but really Joseph suffered a long time. He experienced the pain of abandonment, rejection, slander, and isolation. However, these horrible realities became the premise from which he would lead the greatest nation of the world. His past pain became a platform for him to help guide Egypt and the surrounding nations through seven years of famine. When his brothers, who had sold him into slavery, came before him in Egypt, he lovingly provided for them because he understood that his pain had a purpose. He was even used to save the lives of his father, his abusive brothers, and their families, inviting them to live with him in Egypt. Joseph understood that if he had not been in Egypt, he wouldn't have been positioned to save his father and brothers.

I believe that just as Joseph's painful experiences helped to prepare him for second-in-command leadership in the greatest nation in the world, so also will your past painful experiences empower you to reach teens who desperately need to be connected to hope and possibility. Why not appreciate your past pain and realize that what you had to go through positioned and poised you to reach teens in your community, school, and ministry.

Much of my youth work over the years was built on the pain of my teenage years. Although I was brought up by both of my parents in a loving home, I can still vividly remember some of the very painful experiences from the fifth grade until the eighth grade. I remember being self-conscious, sitting alone in junior high school at lunch, and being called "Big Lips" and "Dumbo." I remember being so torn down by those words that I found it difficult at times even to hold up my head to look at people when I talked to them. I was so self-conscious that I would frequently hold my hands in front of my face when standing in front of people because I believed I was ugly. I remember my pillow being soaked with tears at night as I cried myself to sleep, thinking about all of the painful words hurled my way. Mine was a hard, harsh reality that I've never forgotten.

As an eighth grader, I have never forgotten the pain I experienced when a local television station in the Quad Cities where I grew up broadcasted a false, unflattering exposé about my father and the church he founded and led as pastor. The ridicule that followed from my peers was relentless. For many months after the false report was aired on television, groups of students would make cross signs at me with their fingers and walk to the other side of the hallway at school as I passed them. I hated walking through the hallways because I had to endure this treatment every day. I remember many times sitting down to eat lunch in the cafeteria, only to have all of the students get up and move to another table. I ate alone for countless days because of the cruelty of many students. Being isolated and ostracized week after week felt horrible. That year was one of the most painful times of my life.

I now realize that there was great purpose in those painful experiences. All of these years later, those painful experiences have created the capacity in me to connect with lonely and dejected teens who are going through their own struggles—just like I did. Those experiences helped to build a platform for me to reach troubled, hurting, and self-conscious teens today. I understand their pain because I experienced hurts in my past. Just like there was a purpose for my pain, there is also a purpose in your pain. Try to do what I have done. Allow your own painful experiences to drive you to make a difference in the lives of teens today!

FIRE IS GREATER THAN FUNDING

Years ago coal-powered locomotives pulled trains across the country. These locomotives were able to generate enough power through combustion of the coal to pull heavy boxcars for hundreds of miles. The combustion process caused the coal to be converted into energy that ultimately powered the loco-motives.

Along a similar line of thinking, when your past pains are converted into a sense of purpose, passion is produced in you! *Passion* is the "fire" that is needed to make a difference in the lives of teens on a consistent basis. I call that passion "the internal inferno" because an *inferno* is a large fire that is hard to control. I am not speaking of a literal inferno but rather of an inner inferno of passion that should drive you to regularly empower youth. This passion pushes you to keep engaging them in spite of what you encounter as you try to reach them. Passion is greater than excitement because ex-citement fluctuates. Passion is like being ignited with a flame that won't burn out. This invisible force of energy called pas-sion mobilizes you to make a difference in the lives of teens. This passion is oftentimes derived from the painful ordeals of the past that have been converted into efforts to positively impact youth today.

Passion is that special "fire" in a person's soul that converts into outgoing energy and effort to connect with teens—regard-less of costs or requirements. The fire of passion in you drives you to do something worthwhile; it moves you to make a dif-ference. That passion energizes you to pick teens up, take them out to eat, hang out with them, play ball with them, walk the mall with them, show up to their programs and games, tutor them, take them on trips, act goofy with them, and so much more! Passion is that indescribable inner combustion that mo-tivates you to reach them. You must have this fire to enable you to pull through seasons of discouragement, disappointment, and even the lack of program funding.

Funding does not and cannot take the place of passion and drive in youth work. I have seen many good people with great ideas for reaching the youth, but they lacked the passion to follow through with their ideas. Their lack of fire was attributed to the guise of the claim that funding was needed in order to start making a difference in the lives of teens. Rather than starting with what they had and expanding as funding increased, they lost valuable time because they were solely focused on funding. In some instances, the funding was never obtained, so the youth work was never initiated.

A strong work ethic is an indispensable quality in youth work. The youth worker must have grit and tenacity to consistently reach out to teens with or without funds. Youth workers must be willing to do the work of youth engagement when the youth program is in its infancy stages. They must be willing to knock on doors, pass out flyers, plan youth sessions, meet with principals of schools, volunteer at schools, go to youth work seminars, and even invest their own funds in their vision. The energy to reach youth comes from the fire that's in one's soul—not from the funds that are in one's hands.

Funding is often the great illusion of youth work. I've heard people say, "When we get the funding, we will do this or that." I have seen non-profit organizations with unlimited funds at their disposal do little or nothing among the youth in their communities. Money wasn't the issue; the lack of passion was the issue. Some of them were so comfortable with their salaries, benefits, and office spaces that they lacked the drive to actually engage the teens of the community they were supposedly there to reach. Subsequently, hundreds of thousands and sometimes millions of dollars later, the teens in those communities were still not engaged. This issue is pervasive in many areas. Many entities with adequate funding are not able to convert those funds into quantifiable and evidenced-based results in the communities that they serve.

Results among our youth cannot solely be measured by the size of grants, program buildings, or budgets. The results must be measured by the action of those organizations among our teens. Are the organizations with the funding driven by passionate youth workers who get out among the teens to engage them in a way that produces measurable results that positively affect the communities?

If you are just launching your youth work efforts or program, remember this: action creates momentum; money doesn't! Some people believe that obtaining a tax-exempt status from the Internal Revenue Service and a 501(c)(3) designation is everything. Indeed, this status is important because the organization is positioned to receive charitable donations and grants that can aid growth, but this designation is not everything. This tax-exempt designation won't put the fire in you or awaken you in the wee hours of the morning with new ideas on how to reach youth. A 501(c)(3) designation won't drive you to sacrifice your time to hang out with teens in your neighborhood or to spend a Saturday passing out your program flyers. A tax exemption won't put that twinkle in your eye every time you discuss your program. These motivations only come from having the fire to make a difference. As you start your program, make sure you maintain your fire to make a difference!

Grantors and funders prefer to support passionate people with plans rather than plans that lack passionate people to carry them out. They may not say this directly, but they want to know if you and your organization have the fire. They will ask questions such as:

- "What have you or your organization done in the last few years without funding?"
- "How many teens have you reached?"
- "Are you driven by a sense of mission that is greater than your desire for funding?"

I encourage you to passionately initiate your youth work efforts even without funds because your "fire" is what reaches teens and will cause people to take notice. Start moving forward because people love to support individuals and programs that are already on the move. Remember that your passionate work without funding is an indicator of how you will work when you do receive funding.

When I first began Operation Link-Up in 1996, everyone on our team had the fire. What we lacked in funding was compensated for by our collective passion to make a difference in the lives of teens. We stretched the minimal resources and did what we could do with what we had. We were blessed in those years with an incredible team of unpaid youth workers who were committed to engaging youth in the Brainerd and Marquette Park neighborhoods of Chicago. They volunteered their time on a weekly basis as we strived to accomplish the vision of Operation Link-Up. They went far beyond the call of duty.

Two team members from those early years had an extraordinary passion to reach teens. Carrie Simpson started working for Operation Link-Up in the early 2000s, completing secretarial tasks during the day and then tutoring the teens during afterschool hours. She exhibited a great amount of patience with all of the teens in our program—particularly with the behaviorally challenged. If they were angry, she could talk them down, getting them to open up and share their feelings with her. The youth loved her, and she passionately loved them.

Carrie possessed a relentless work ethic, arriving at work an hour early and remaining until most of the teens left in the evening. She performed all of her duties in spite of her own challenges. Because of her cerebral palsy, walking was sometimes a struggle for her. Although she had crutches to assist her, some days were more difficult than others.

One day she told me about the unbelievable challenges she had faced during the earlier years of her life. She had been abandoned in squalor as a disabled baby and was socially castigated as a handicapped child. Her peers belittled her because of her disabilities. However, none of those negatives stopped her! She overcame seemingly insurmountable odds and obtained her bachelor's degree from a state university. Her story of resilience and determination helped me to understand why she was so driven to help teens. Her painful experiences enabled her to relate easily to the ostracized and marginalized teens who walked through our doors. She had that special fire and drive that distinguished her from everyone else on our team.

Reginald "Rocky" Robertson began working at Operation Link-Up as the leader of our martial arts program in the mid-2000's. I recall how driven he was to make a difference in the lives of teens on his first interview. A very unassuming man, he wore extremely thick glasses and didn't really look like a martial arts specialist. However, he held multiple belts and certifications in the world of martial arts.

After he began, I soon found out that he was driven by his passion to help teens, arriving an hour before his martial arts sessions to prepare for them. After the sessions were over, he would remain for an additional hour or two to assist in other parts of the program. Whenever I asked him to assist me in mentoring teens in local public schools, he would happily assist. Whenever I needed his help for outings, I could count on him to be there. When chaperones were needed for overnight trips, he helped. Reginald was so much more than a martial arts instructor; he was driven to do whatever he could to make a difference.

One day after the programs had ended, when only he and I were in the office, I decided to ask him why he was so passionate about working with teens. His answer literally blew me away! I sat in my office in utter disbelief as he shared that he had been born legally blind. As a result of his visual disability, he was classified as a special education student, labeled as learning disabled, and relegated to classrooms with students who suffered with severe cognitive disabilities. He explained that the designation was difficult for him to accept because he should have been placed in the more advanced classrooms.

As a child, he had spent his summers at the Camp for the Blind in Missouri. He shared that he often felt left out, isolated, and misunderstood because of his visual disability. However, learning martial arts helped transform him and gave him hope in his late teenage years. He went on to serve in the Peace Corps of the United States, as well as to obtain an associate of arts degree. As I listened to him share about his past that night, his passion began to make sense to me. I realized that his past pain was what fueled him to serve so selflessly in our program.

Both Carrie and Reginald were passionate partly because of their own painful experiences. Both of them stood on the platforms of their painful pasts and used them to make a difference. Instead of living in self-pity, they found purpose in their past pain, converting their hurts into seemingly endless energy to serve the next generation. Their purpose and passion drove them to show up early and stay late during the early years of our youth program. They had exactly what it took to reach teens in Chicago; they had the fire!

USE THE POWER OF YOUR PLATFORM

Your platform is a composite of your past experiences. No doubt, these experiences have helped to shape your perspective. Making the most of everything you've been through is so important. One of the ways to do this is to use the platform of your past experiences to impact the teens today. Stand boldly on the platform of your experiences and pour wisdom, insight, and understanding into the hearts and minds of teens. All of your experiences have prepared you for this stage of positive youth engagement. I encourage you to maximize the power of your platform as a champion, a coach, and a counselor to the teens around you.

AS A CHAMPION…

Almost every great champion in the sport of boxing was knocked down at least one time. What made them great was their picking themselves up and continuing to fight. In life, a champion is someone who has overcome adversity. Maybe you were knocked down by an eating disorder, academic failure, sexual abuse, dropping out of school, depression, suicide attempts, sexual promiscuity, drug addiction, criminal activities, or even incarceration. Share how you got up after these issues knocked you down! You may have taken years to get back up, but the fact that you did get up is all that matters, for that getting up is what makes you a champion. Let them know that your struggles were (and sometimes still are) real. No longer do you need to be embarrassed about what knocked you down in the past. Whatever happened served a great purpose in preparing you for this moment to reach the next generation.

Being incognito and trying to reach teens is impossible; it just doesn't work. You have to take off the mask and makeup. Teens want to know if you are a "believable hero" or one who is full of talk and rhetoric. Therefore, sharing with them about some of the battles you've been through is very necessary. Show them some of your "battle scars." By that, I mean help them see the contrast between what you used to be then and what you are now. Showing them pictures and telling them how messed up you were when you were addicted is allowable but also show how sober you now are. Telling them how aimless you were as a high school dropout but how proud you now are because of completing your education is acceptable. Sharing how hopeless you felt when you were incarcerated and how grateful you are to be free is certainly permissible. Telling them about how lonely and depressed you used to be and how connected and happy you are now is also acceptable.

Maybe your battle scars are different than some of the ones I mentioned, but please don't cover them, remove the mask and makeup. Your story of victory will give your teens hope and help them to realize that if you made it through hard times, they can too. Secondly, your struggles will help them to see that you can relate to their present struggles and battles. Therefore, as you take the time to share your battle scars by telling your stories of struggle and success, you will inspire them to fight on and not give up. Please remember that the grounds of your success were fertilized by your failure. Every struggle of your past helped to prepare you for your present assignment to effectively engage teens!

As a Coach…

Great coaches propel others to excellence. As you coach teens, use the wisdom attained from your past experiences to help them excel. Winning coaches have an extraordinary vision of possibilities for their students and/or athletes, so they see the possibilities of what can be in the lives of the teens. As the motivating force in their lives, you can help those possibilities become realities. In sports, most coaches urge their athletes to stretch their muscles before competitions so the athletes will be loose and limber when competing.

As a teen life coach, "stretching" the teens in your home, school, ministry and neighborhood is incredibly important. Challenge them to be better, push them past mediocrity, incentivize their future successes, and expose them to the next level. You may need to sacrifice being liked by them as you hold them accountable and require their maximum efforts at all times.

As you coach teens into success, make sure you only speak positive words over them. Never demean them verbally; only uplift them. I believe that you will see what you decree over them. A decree is "a verbal order that is usually legal in nature." In the court of law, judges usually make decrees (or judgments) that carry great legal weight. So as their coach, understand that your words also carry great weight. If you call them the right name long enough, they will answer to it and even perform at that level. Call your teens "champ," "winner," "king" or "queen," "genius," "superstar" and any other positive name you can think of! Never call them "stupid," "slow," "dumb," or "ignorant." Remember, whatever they hear the most, they will believe. Be a coach who speaks life and possibility into them. They will most certainly live up or down to whatever you call them, so speak the right words over them!

Don't let losses cause you to give up. In the sports world,

great coaches don't win every game, but they teach their players how to come back from losses by making the necessary adjustments to win the next time. Please remember that when your teens go through those losing streaks attitudinally, academically, and behaviorally, you must not give up on them. In fact, use their losses to prepare them for future victories. Use their lowest moments as teachable moments. Don't beat them over the head with what they did wrong; rather, talk to them about how to do it better the next time. Help them to write a game plan on how to conquer that problem area the next time.

After they have suffered defeats, be sure to tell them "You're my winner!" Call them "my champions" after they have not been or done their best. Be the coach who holds onto your teens when they are "losing" and rejoices with them when they are "winning." They will learn how to win spiritually, academically, and socially as they develop into the champions you always knew they could become.

AS A COUNSELOR...

Try to be a go-to person who will provide teens with meaningful advice and guidance. As teens navigate the tricky terrain of their teenage years, they are often full of questions about all types of issues. Therefore, they need to be able to seek out insight from trusted adults. Unlike many adults who often "seek advice" after their minds are already made up about matters, teens are often open-minded when they ask for advice. Try to provide that "safe space and place" where they can be heard without being castigated or judged for their feelings. You may not always have the answers for them, and many times you may not agree with them. However, hearing them is so important so they will, in turn, be willing to hear your perspective. Your guidance will never fall on deaf ears if your ears are open to their cries for conversation and understanding.

Strive to be a trusted, objective voice in the lives of your teens so that you can help shape their opinions and views. Too many teens are steered by peer pressure and pop culture. Coupling this pressure with the fact that many of them have strained relationships with their parents can raise the possibility of missteps and bad decisions. I have seen some teens literally shut out their parents. They avoid speaking with their parents. This avoidance can be dangerous because teens who have minimal dialogue with their parents tend to gravitate toward peers who share their opinions. Sometimes seeking the advice of peers is for the worst.

Your role as an objective third party in the lives of teens can be so helpful. When they are not getting along with their parents, you can still provide healthy and sound advice to guide them through those times. Teens can greatly benefit from healthy "outside adult voices" who can direct them toward positive decisions and actions. I am not saying that you should try to take the place of their parents; rather, seek to be a supplement to parents. When they are going through difficult times with their teens, try to be that positive third party who helps the teens with sound advice and support that any concerned parent would appreciate.

The following are a few key points to consider about being a counselor to youth:

1. Keep an open mind.

2. Maintain confidentiality because nothing ruins trust more than loose lips.

3. Always be willing to listen. Listen far more than you talk.

4. "Listen" with your eyes and body language—not just your ears. In other words "be tuned" in to them.

5. If some teens have difficulty verbalizing their feelings, ask them to write, draw or even paint what they feel.

6. If you have one-on-one conversations, make sure it's never behind closed doors (unless they are your children). If in an office or another facility, try to make sure you are both visible to others.

7. Be very careful about ending your talks with hugs. Personally, I would advise against physical contact unless you are close relatives.

8. If you feel that more advanced and/or professional counseling is needed, try to discuss this consideration with them and their parents.

THINK IT THROUGH

1. Describe a painful ordeal you experienced in your childhood or teenage years.

_____

_____

_____

_____

2. How can you use your own painful experience to connect with youth today?

_____

_____

_____

_____

3. Perhaps you know of some teens who are struggling attitudinally, academically, or spiritually. In what ways can you help coach them through this tough period?

_____

_____

_____

_____

CHAPTER SIX

BUILD CONNECTIONS

CREATE A SPACE
WHERE YOUTH CAN PLUG IN

FOR TEENS TO be able to find a place where they can escape is important. Many of them are constantly bombarded with negativity, whether it's in their mind, in their home, or among their peers. Negativity, which often has an adverse physiological effect on teens, causes depression, fatigue, and lack of motivation. I have mentored dozens of teens over the years who were attempting to navigate negative home environments. Sometimes the negativity and tension stemmed from conflict between their parents or between the teen and the live-in friend of a parent. The negativity in their homes was incredibly stressful to them.

I have had to comfort teens who were being emotionally and physically battered by intoxicated loved ones. Some teens have been so terribly traumatized by gang activity and gun violence on their blocks or in their apartment buildings, that they could hardly sleep at night. Some teens have been so food deprived, they suffered from constant headaches. In an effort not to feel their throbbing headaches, they would resort to sleeping most of the time. I could list many other negative teen scenarios that have helped me to understand that one purpose of the Operation Link-Up Teen Center is to be a place where teens can plug in to peace. Therefore, I established and strictly enforce a positivity zone on our premises at all times. No form of negativity is permitted inside the facility. Negative talk, vibes, and energy are not tolerated because most of the teens in our program are trying to escape from that habitual negativism. The Center is a place of peace, positivity, and rest!

If you have ever travelled through airports, you have probably seen the phone-charging outlet stations strategically placed throughout the concourses for easy access. They are welcome sights to travelers whose phone batteries have died. Eager travelers rush to the charging outlets, connect their phones, and then wait for the batteries to be recharged. One of the ways the person knows that the batteries are being adequately recharged is by the battery power indicator known as a bar. As their phone batteries grow stronger, more bars are visible on the screen of their phones. A phone connected to a charging outlet can take anywhere from a few minutes to an hour to fully charge its battery. These charging outlet stations are vital to air travelers. Having no charging outlet stations in the airports would have an adverse effect on many travelers if they couldn't recharge their phone batteries.

Many teenagers are emotionally drained, tired, frustrated, and fatigued—like cell phone batteries. They need charging stations in their communities to plug in to. Some of them feel hopeless and helpless because of the negative realities that surround them. The dysfunctions and negativity around them have drained their desires and dreams. Subsequently, some of them are lethargic and basically go through the motions of daily life without passion or purpose. Their batteries are drained; they have no bars on their "emotional screens."

Educator and Youth Worker, creating a space where they can plug into peace and positivity is important. Whether that place is in your home, school, or organization, maintain an atmosphere charged with positive conversations, affirmations, music, pictures on the walls, and so forth. Create a space that brings peace and calm to their souls. Establish a place where they can chill out, learn, share, and grow. These kinds of spaces have a profound positive effect on teens, regardless of the negative circumstances they have to face when they leave your program or presence.

The positive energy of your meeting space can help to transform their attitudes and behavior. They may be emotionally drained when they come to you, but do all that you can do to charge their batteries and raise their emotional bars. Let the love, comfort, and warmth of your meeting space charge them. Let your pats on their backs, fist bumps, and nods of acknowledgment charge them. Let loving honesty, constructive criticism, and your candid conversations charge them. Let the peace in your meeting space raise their bars of hope high enough for them to see the great potential and possibilities in their futures! They may come to you drained, but they should leave you charged by the faith, hope, and love they experience while in your space.

Years ago at Operation Link-Up, my team and I had promoted a summer event called the Men's Round Table for teen and young adult males. Our objective was to discuss effective strategies on how to handle their anger issues. The event was attended by twenty to twenty-five young men. They sat and listened intently as my team and I discussed many of the triggers that had historically angered young men. We then equipped them with practical everyday tools they could apply to their daily lives in an effort to control their anger issues. Different attendees mentioned various experiences that had made them angry in the past. Most of them highlighted strained relationships with their fathers and generational poverty issues as sources of great frustration and anger. Several of them shared these issues with tears streaming down their faces.

My team and I were deeply touched to see these young men with such tough exteriors become so vulnerable and openly emotional. Following our time of sharing, we prayed together and enjoyed a delicious dinner. When we dismissed the session, I followed my usual routine of shaking hands, saying goodnight with a high five, or hugging each of them as they left the building.

After the young men had left, one member of my staff said, "Rev. Lee, that was a miracle."

I didn't quite understand, so he explained that most of the

young men in attendance were members of two rival gangs who had been at war with each other on the southwest side of Chicago. The two gangs were the predominantly Hispanic Ambrose and the predominantly African-American Gangster Disciples. What shocked me the most was when my staff informed me that the young men who were present that evening were probably *packing* (carrying guns). You would not have known that gun-toting rival gangs were present by the way they interacted.

I believe the real miracle took place after that Men's Round Table gathering. The war between the Ambrose and Gangster Disciples completely dissipated, and a truce was called by several of the young men who had attended our anger resolution session. Many of those young men had been drained by the streets and the nonstop negativity of their gangbanging life-styles. However, being connected to a peaceful and positive environment calmed them enough to take a step back from their gang war. That experience taught me never to underestimate the power of a positive environment because it can have a transformative effect on youth.

THREE TYPES OF YOUTH PROGRAMS THAT CONNECT

Communities need various types of youth programs to connect with teens. Each program serves a particular purpose. Some programs are started because a family is composed of several teenagers, and the parents end up connecting with their own teenagers and their teenagers' friends in their home. Some programs start as the result of adults' having a desire to provide a safe space for youth to gather in a geographical area, such as a neighborhood or in a multi-family complex. Other programs start when a team of adults organize to accomplish a mission among a particular demographic of teens in a targeted area. Regardless of how a program starts, what is of utmost importance is for it to be a positive place where teens feel connected. The following are three types of teen programs that can serve as great connection points for teens in a community.

A SAFE PLACE

This type of program is not very formal or structured but is a great place for teens to hang out. A safe place youth program is usually grass roots in nature. These types of programs are frequently led by one or two passionate adults who allow youth to gather in their homes or in meeting rooms. These programs are really safe havens in various communities. Many times no written records or formalized corporate mission is involved, but passionate adults are present for the teens. These adults often spend their own money to serve the youth because they don't apply for outside funding.

Safe place youth programs are greatly beneficial in communities because all teens are usually welcome and there is no criteria to join. These programs have a "homey" feeling of warmth and love. Having a formal agenda is a secondary priority in these types of programs. On any day when the youth gather, they may enjoy a variety of things because there may or may not be an agenda. These group gatherings may involve hanging out and talking, playing video games, enjoying good home-cooked food, resolving a neighborhood issue, or even planning for a future trip to an amusement park.

These programs are lifelines for the youth in many communities. Sometimes they are most effective since they typically do not have any formalities and protocols. The adults who lead them may not even desire to formalize their program by obtaining a tax I.D. number, incorporating, and opening a program bank account. These programs are often self-funded by the adults who lead them. In these informal yet effective youth gathering spots, countless numbers of teens feel emotionally safe and loved by caring adults.

A STABLE PLACE

This type of program functions with a specific focal point. A Stable Place Program usually has an ongoing narrative with participating youth about a particular subject. Youth who participate in these types of programs know exactly what they are going to get when they show up. Some examples of Stable Place Programs include programs for tutoring, music, sports, performing arts, martial arts, computer technology, arts and crafts. These programs are usually organized and have consistent practices.

Agendas and plans are usually set far in advance so the programming may be consistent and effective. The adults who oversee these programs have usually mastered the subject matter and are eager to develop the skills of young people taking them. They are usually somewhat less engaging about the day-to-day matters in the lives of participating youth because of the time constraints on sessions and lessons.

These programs help teens gain a mastery in specific areas of interest. Therefore, the objective of these programs is streamlined and result-oriented. Participation in these programs usually requires a teen to formally sign up and pay a fee for continued participation. Stable Place Youth Programs help to develop the gifts and talents of many teens every week. These programs often lay the foundation for teens to reach higher levels of excellence and mastery in the future. Most Stable Place Programs, which are formally organized and incorporated, are often a part of larger associations. Some of them are even franchises.

A Systematic Place

Systematic Programs are very defined and refined, with everything handled in an established manner. Most of these programs have been around for a while and have mastered their operational systems. They are usually incorporated and have obtained state and federal non-profit status. Often funded through public and private grants, as well as contracts and private donors, they frequently offer a wide variety of teen empowerment opportunities within their overall program.

Participation in these types of programs usually requires teens to complete a formal enrollment process. These programs are pattern-driven, so curriculum and session plans are the norm. Systematic Programs are usually staffed by people who specialize in youth work or are formally trained to work with youth, the youth ministry, youth advocacy, counseling, education, etc.

Systematic Programs are comprehensive and are able to impact teens in a variety of ways. For instance, this type of program may offer character development, trade apprentice-ships, performing arts, counseling, and social justice engage-ment in one location. These programs often have so many areas of engagement that the lives of participating teens can revolve around the high volume of activities offered. These programs often serve as the primary activity point for teens outside of their homes and schools.

Systematic youth programs are extremely beneficial to the communities they serve. The structure of these programs often positions them to obtain funding more easily for their daily operations. Many communities benefit from having these programs because these programs are able to provide wraparound youth services and collaborations with other in-stitutions.

BE THE BRIDGE

Many teens have lofty dreams and desires, but many of them settle for mediocrity because they are without bridges to help them cross over into greater levels of progress and success. Bridges enable people and automobiles to cross over bodies of water and other obstacles. They also serve as connections be-tween pieces of land. If there were no bridges, our routines and travel patterns would be greatly altered. I don't think most people would like to have to swim or catch a boat across small bodies of water because there were no functional bridges. Yet every day, teens with great purpose and potential simply cannot find bridges to help them cross over to greater opportunities and open doors. Therefore, adults must embrace the responsibility of being bridges into betterment for young men and women.

I learned this truth about being a bridge many years ago when I first began working with youth on the south side of Chicago. What I didn't initially realize was that the youth I served saw me as much more than a youth program director. Many of them saw me as a way out of their troubles and struggles. At first, I did not wholeheartedly accept the immense responsibility of becoming a bridge for them. Becoming a bridge meant that I had to sacrifice my time and energy so I could connect them to greater opportunities. I would always have to keep my eyes and ears open for things that could benefit them. I felt compelled to help them cross over into better opportunities.

Becoming a bridge for them entailed my organizing college tours to connect them to the possibilities of higher learning and campus living. Sometimes being a bridge meant taking them away from the big city of Chicago on youth retreats in rural areas to connect them to the tranquility of silence and a slower pace. Sometimes being a bridge meant my staff and me taking them on free overnight trips to three- and four-star hotels to connect them to upscale lodging and amenities. Sometimes being a bridge was organizing large youth rallies followed by intentionally scheduled late night parties afterward to connect them to clean, positive fun after dark.

I also learned that my character and credibility had to become a bridge to help them to cross-over into employment opportunities. As Operation Link-Up grew on the southwest side of Chicago, our program attracted many young men. In fact, for every young woman in our program, we had three to four young men. Many of these young men were from economically deprived single-parent homes; therefore, many of them wanted to make money the right way by working a job, as opposed to selling drugs in the community.

My heart was deeply touched by the sad fact that most of them lacked the transportation to get to job sites to fill out applications. They also lacked the appropriate attire to wear to an interview. These factors lessened the probability of their being hired. However, I learned to leverage my relationships with local business establishments in the community where our youth center was located. I realized that my attitude and disposition with the managers at those establishments could actually open the doors of opportunity for the teens in my program. I became very intentional about building genuine relationships with the store owners and managers. As time passed, I was able to recommend many young men from Operation Link-Up for jobs at their establishments. Most of the young men I recommended were hired on the spot without having to go through the formal interview process at various national franchises. I connected would-be employees with employers by following these steps:

1. I would simply tell the managers about the young men I was recommending.

2. I would arrange a time to bring them to the store to introduce them to the managers.

3. After the formal introductions, the mangers would tell them what day to come in and start their new jobs.

Seeing the joy on the face of each young man as he was connected to employment opportunities was always an awesome experience for me. This informal employment referral system taught me the importance of building relationships that enabled my young people to walk over into betterment. I am so grateful for the privilege that I have had to be a bridge to employment opportunities for many teens through the years.

Even though the demands of being a bridge are great, I encourage you to be such a bridge. Sometimes you will hardly be noticed as teens run over you and walk over you. Bridges are often taken for granted and not appreciated. However, none of us can live without them—especially our teens. Some teens will only fulfill their potential when concerned parents, educators, coaches, and pastors become bridges for them to cross over.

I encourage you to build connections that can benefit the teens around you because some of them have been wrongly prejudged and thus denied opportunities. Your character and credibility may be the only bridge that a teen has to connect them to a better future. Your word of recommendation may be all that's needed to connect them to a whole new world of possibility. Always remember that the purpose of your efforts should be to connect teens to higher levels of opportunity and success. As you connect them to opportunities, please know that you will experience blessings because you were their bridge.

THINK IT THROUGH

1. How can you create a positive environment that reinvigorates and encourages youth in your community?

_____

_____

_____

_____

2. If you lead a youth program, what type is it? A safe place, a stable place, or a systematic place?

_____

_____

_____

_____

3. How can you and/or your organization be a bridge to greater opportunities for the youth you serve?

_____

_____

_____

_____

CHAPTER SEVEN

PICTURES, PRAYERS
AND PRACTICAL STRATEGIES

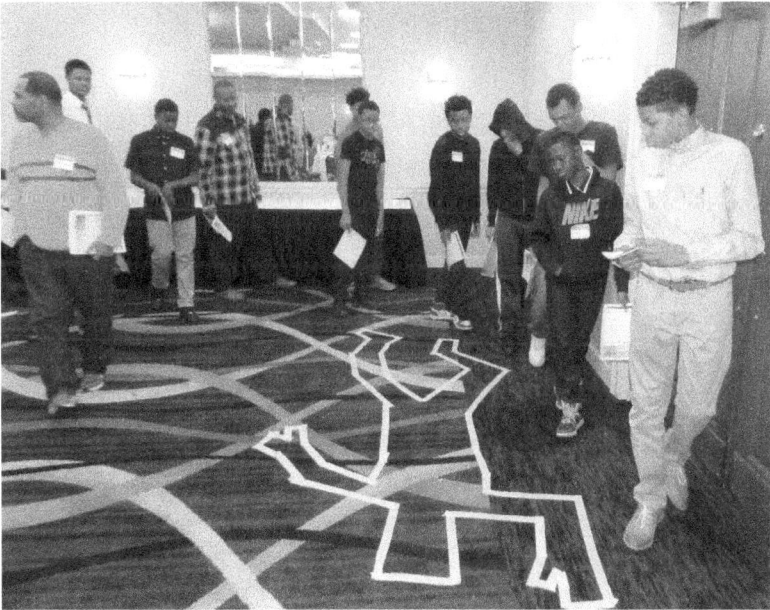

An emotional awareness exercise that we do at O.L.U.
helps youth avoid self-harm and suicide.

Above: These are some of the first youth who came to our after-school mentoring program back in the day.

Below: One of our first after-school youth groups from the southwest side of Chicago who met with us.

Above: My wife, Nedra, is great at teaching young women to embrace their inner and outer beauty.

Below: From the beginning Nedra has helped the vision to reach youth become a reality.

Above: It's always a blast to do breakfast hangouts with the youth.

Below: Some of the youth at O.L.U. studying during an academic assistance session.

Above: Sometimes the O.L.U. youth are hilarious!

Below: Pizza has always been the snack of choice following the afterschool program.

Above: A small group of youth from O.L.U. went swimming on an overnight trip to a hotel.

Below: The youth of O.L.U. pose in front of their limousine in downtown Chicago

Above: Young men show their skills
in an O.L.U. basketball competition.

Below: Some of the skateboarders
at our skateboard competition display their medals.

Above: What a moving moment this was as I prayed for the safety of these youth at one of our rallies!

Below: These guys loved serving elderly people on Saturday mornings.

Above: In this picture, young men from O.L.U. were serving hot meals to community residents.

Below: Young men are always encouraged and empowered at our Rising Star Breakfast events.

*Above:
At times
it's fun just
to be goofy
with teens.*

*Above: Talking about faith and future
with young men is fun.*

Above: One of the O.L.U. micro-mentoring groups, seen here, meets at a public school.

Below: I love teaching life skills to various groups of students.

*Above: Chicago police officers connect with youth
at the O.L.U. Center.*

*Below: Here, I was discussing the senseless murder
of a young person in Chicago with the media.*

Above: Commander Kupczyk and I took this picture after we led a youth peace event in the Eighth District.

Below: One of my joys is training organizations to excel at reaching youth.

PRAYERS TO PRAY OVER TEENS

I encourage you to pray these prayers over the teens in your home and community. I believe that the prayers of adults help to set the stage for success in the lives of teens. Consistent prayer for teens can also help them to avoid pitfalls as they strive to fulfill their potential. In this section, I have included seven categories of prayers to pray for the teens in your life. If you choose to pray about one of the categories each day, I promise it will make a difference in the lives of the teens around you.

See Matthew 7:7-8 and I John 5:14-15 in the Holy Bible as prayer references.

FOUR PRAYERS FOR THEM TO DISCOVER THEIR PURPOSE

God, help them to discover their passions.

God, help them to choose positive paths.

God, help them to avoid distractions.

God, help them to discover and accept Your plan for their lives.

FOUR PRAYERS FOR THEM TO HAVE PEACE

God, help them to think peaceful thoughts.

God, help them not to be stressed out.

God, help them not to be anxious.

God, help them to resolve conflict in a nonviolent manner.

FOUR PRAYERS FOR THEIR PROTECTION

God, protect them from bullying.

God, protect them from self-harm.

God, protect them from all forms of violence.

God, protect them from all forms of addiction.

FOUR PRAYERS FOR THEM TO BE PURE

God, help them to avoid premarital sex.

God, help them to avoid pornography.

God, keep them from any form of prostitution and sex trafficking.

God, keep them from sexual exploitation.

FOUR PRAYERS FOR THEM TO PROGRESS

God, help them to set high goals.

God, help them to progress academically.

God, help them to discover their passions.

God, help them to confidently face challenges.

FOUR PRAYERS FOR THEM TO EXPERIENCE PROMOTION

God, help them to work hard when no one is watching.

God, allow their gifts and talents to be discovered.

God, bless them with opportunities to advance.

God, promote them on their jobs.

FOUR PRAYERS FOR THEM TO HAVE GOOD PARTNERSHIPS

God, help them to choose the right friends.

God, help them to choose good study partners.

God, teach them how to work well with other people.

God, help them to contribute to positive causes.

THREE MONTHS
OF PRACTICAL CONNECTION STRATEGIES

I encourage you to plan how you will connect with teens over the next three months. Map out a strategy on how you will win them. As you engage them, be sure to implement one of the five "I's" each week. The five "I's" in chapter four are as follows:

1. Take an **INTEREST** in them.

2. **INVEST** in them.

3. **INVITE** them.

4. **INSPIRE** them.

5. **INSTRUCT** them.

Plan each engagement, execute it, and then assess it. Following this plan over a three-month period may be all that is needed to build or rebuild strong connections with teens in your home and community.

Plan each youth engagement and make the time to work the plan. If you consistently connect with the teens over the next three months, you may end up birthing a new relationship with your child, a student mentoring group, a teen organization, or a youth ministry. Each time you connect with them, you will be forging deeper bonds of trust and credibility. Remember that initially the youth with whom you are attempting to connect or reconnect may be hesitant and resistant. That's okay; don't take it personally. Be flexible enough to know that they may be unsure of your intentions.

They may wonder in silence or even ask out loud, "Why are you trying to get close all of a sudden?"

Don't take offence; just say something like, "I just want to stay connected to you all." Keep your plans simple and keep proving that your love for them is genuine by continuing to make time for them. You may have to feel your way through some of your initial connection times. For instance, if you take them to their favorite eating spot on week one, they may ask to return to the same place the following week. Don't be too rigid and demand that they do something else with you in a different location. If that's where they feel the most comfortable, keep going there. In fact, it may be the place where they choose to open up and share what's really going on in their lives. In this case, simply go with the flow so you can strengthen the connection.

To increase your credibility with the youth, keep your word and follow through with your plans. Try to do things at the same time as much as possible. After a few weeks of your consistently connecting with them, they may ask to include other friends in your hang-out time. They may start to text and call you during the week to ask what you are going to do next. These will be signs that your connections with the teens are growing. Growing connections doesn't take years to happen; it simply takes committed and consistent adults who care enough to intentionally connect with the teens around them.

I know that you will see amazing results as you connect with the teens in your home and community. Be sure to plan and reflect on your teen engagements each week in the spaces provided on the following pages. Be as thorough as you possibly can. Plan and then execute the activity, and you will make inroads in the lives of your youth. I am so glad you have chosen to be a difference maker in the lives of teens. Go for it!

WEEK ONE
PRACTICAL CONNECTION STRATEGY

Choose an "I"

_____ Interest in them.   _____ Inspire them.

_____ Invest in them.   _____ Instruct them.

_____ Invite them.

What Will You Do?

_____

_____

_____

_____

_____

How Did It Go?

_____

_____

_____

_____

_____

Next Steps

_____

_____

_____

Week Two
Practical Connection Strategy

Choose an "I"

____ Interest in them. ____ Inspire them.

____ Invest in them. ____ Instruct them.

____ Invite them.

What Will You Do?

_____

_____

_____

_____

_____

How Did It Go?

_____

_____

_____

_____

_____

Next Steps

_____

_____

_____

WEEK THREE
PRACTICAL CONNECTION STRATEGY

Choose an "I"

____ Interest in them.	____ Inspire them.
____ Invest in them.	____ Instruct them.
____ Invite them.	

What Will You Do?

_____

_____

_____

_____

_____∾

How Did It Go?

_____

_____

_____

_____

_____∾

Next Steps

_____

_____

_____∾

WEEK FOUR
PRACTICAL CONNECTION STRATEGY

Choose an "I"

_____ Interest in them.   _____ Inspire them.

_____ Invest in them.   _____ Instruct them.

_____ Invite them.

What Will You Do?

_____

_____

_____

_____

_____ ❧

How Did It Go?

_____

_____

_____

_____

_____ ❧

Next Steps

_____

_____

_____ ❧

Week Five
Practical Connection Strategy

Choose an "I"

_____ Interest in them.   _____ Inspire them.

_____ Invest in them.   _____ Instruct them.

_____ Invite them.

What Will You Do?

_____

_____

_____

_____

_____

How Did It Go?

_____

_____

_____

_____

_____

Next Steps

_____

_____

_____

WEEK SIX
PRACTICAL CONNECTION STRATEGY

Choose an "I"

_____ Interest in them.   _____ Inspire them.

_____ Invest in them.   _____ Instruct them.

_____ Invite them.

What Will You Do?

_____

_____

_____

_____

_____

How Did It Go?

_____

_____

_____

_____

_____

Next Steps

_____

_____

_____

Week Seven
Practical Connection Strategy

Choose an "I"

_____ Interest in them.   _____ Inspire them.

_____ Invest in them.   _____ Instruct them.

_____ Invite them.

What Will You Do?

_____

_____

_____

_____

_____

How Did It Go?

_____

_____

_____

_____

_____

Next Steps

_____

_____

_____

Week Eight
Practical Connection Strategy

Choose an "I"

_____ Interest in them.   _____ Inspire them.

_____ Invest in them.   _____ Instruct them.

_____ Invite them.

What Will You Do?

_____

_____

_____

_____

_____

How Did It Go?

_____

_____

_____

_____

_____

Next Steps

_____

_____

_____

WEEK NINE
PRACTICAL CONNECTION STRATEGY

Choose an "I"

_____ Interest in them.   _____ Inspire them.

_____ Invest in them.   _____ Instruct them.

_____ Invite them.

What Will You Do?

_____

_____

_____

_____

_____

How Did It Go?

_____

_____

_____

_____

_____

Next Steps

_____

_____

_____

WEEK TEN
PRACTICAL CONNECTION STRATEGY

Choose an "I"

_____ Interest in them.   _____ Inspire them.

_____ Invest in them.   _____ Instruct them.

_____ Invite them.

What Will You Do?

_____

_____

_____

_____

_____

How Did It Go?

_____

_____

_____

_____

_____

Next Steps

_____

_____

_____

Week Eleven
Practical Connection Strategy

Choose an "I"

_____ Interest in them.   _____ Inspire them.

_____ Invest in them.   _____ Instruct them.

_____ Invite them.

What Will You Do?

_____

_____

_____

_____

_____

How Did It Go?

_____

_____

_____

_____

_____

Next Steps

_____

_____

_____

WEEK TWELVE
PRACTICAL CONNECTION STRATEGY

Choose an "I"

_____ Interest in them.   _____ Inspire them.

_____ Invest in them.   _____ Instruct them.

_____ Invite them.

What Will You Do?

_____

_____

_____

_____

_____

How Did It Go?

_____

_____

_____

_____

_____

Next Steps

_____

_____

_____

Week Thirteen
Practical Connection Strategy

Choose an "I"

____ Interest in them.   ____ Inspire them.

____ Invest in them.   ____ Instruct them.

____ Invite them.

What Will You Do?

_____

_____

_____

_____

_____

How Did It Go?

_____

_____

_____

_____

_____

Next Steps

_____

_____

_____

www.ingramcontent.com/pod-product-compliance
Lightning Source LLC
Chambersburg PA
CBHW050734030426
42336CB00012B/1565